FEDERATION

Lena River

Lake Baikal

Amur River

Onon R.

Qolen Lake (Hulur)

Mau (Evil) Heights

Buura steppe

Kerulen River (Herlen)

Ralga R. (Halkin)

Bayur L. (Buyr)

MANCHURIA

Orgon R.

Ulaan-Baatar

Senggur R.

Tuula R.

Dungchang (Mukden)

Qara-qorum (Hahorun) established 1335

OLIA

B I

Sondeiwu (Xuanhua)

Chabchiyal Pass (Juyong Guan)

Kalgan (Zhangjiakou)

Jungdu (Beijing)

YELLOW

SEA

Huang He (Hwang Ho)

Huang He (Yellow River)

HAN

oko Lake (Qinghai Hu)

Old course of Huang He

Namging (Kaifeng)

N

A

EAST CHINA SEA

CHINGGIS KHAN

The Golden History
of the Mongols

Chinggis Khan

The Golden
CHINGGIS
History of
KHAN
The Mongols

translated and with an
introduction by
Urgunge Onon

revised by
Sue Bradbury

LONDON THE FOLIO SOCIETY
1993

© The Folio Society Ltd, 1993

Set in Sabon by Selwood Systems
Midsomer Norton
Printed at The Bath Press, Avon
on Hamilton Wove paper
and bound by them in full cloth
printed with the Mongolian title
drawn by the author
and the English title
drawn by John Andrew
Typography by Bernard Roberts

Second printing 1994

CONTENTS

ILLUSTRATIONS

With the exception of the first and last plates, all illustrations are reproduced from the fourteenth-century History of the Mongols *by Rashid al-Din, by permission of the Bibliothèque Nationale, Paris*

INTRODUCTION

THE EAST HAS KNOWN THREE TRULY GREAT
men. The first was Sakyamuni, born a prince in about 500
BC, in what is now Nepal. Distressed by human suffering, he
left his family and achieved enlightenment through medi-
tation, becoming the Buddha. According to his teachings, life
is painful, the origin of pain is desire, the end of pain can be
achieved by ending desire, and the way to this is through right
living. This philosophy of 'cause and effect' spread northward
into Tibet, where it absorbed the local religion and changed
greatly in its nature. The resulting synthesis, known as
Lamaism, can be criticised for its passivity and fatalism: nevertheless Lamaism became popular among the Mongols during
the reign of Qubilai Khan (1260–1294).

The second great man of the East was Confucius, born at
around the same time as the Buddha, into China's lower
aristocracy. Confucius wanted to restore China to a golden
age of peace. He also said that 'the universe belongs to the
people', but although he emphasised the importance of ethical
conduct at all levels of society, he believed implicitly that
that society should be shaped by the hereditary rights of
aristocrats. He helped endow the Chinese with the idea that
China lay at the centre of the universe; and he persuaded the
ordinary people to confine their loyalties to their family and
the emperor. Confucianism spread to the countries of the East
that practised settled agriculture, but not to nomadic countries
like Mongolia.

The third great man of the East was Temujin, the personal
name of Chinggis Khan. Chinggis was born on the sixteenth
day of the fourth lunar month in the year 1162, into the
family of a tribal leader. Some historians — for example
the Persian Rashid al-Din (1247–1318), who was of Jewish
origin — maintain that Chinggis was born earlier, in 1155,
the Year of the Pig. Neither Jews nor Muslims (nor, for that
matter, Mongols) like pigs, and many Persians deeply hated
the Mongols, who set up a dynasty (the Il-Khan, which ran
from 1265 to 1335) in their country. So it was probably with
some satisfaction that Rashid al-Din determined 1155 as

the year of birth of the Mongol world-conqueror. It *is* true, however, that Chinggis died in 1227, also a Pig Year.

Mongol society developed in three stages. It was established on the basis of a hunting economy in the forest regions to the north of the Mongol heartland. During this period the title *mergen* was created, meaning 'a good hunter' or 'an intelligent person'. When the Mongols emerged from the forests, they created a new title, *ba'atur*, or 'hero', which indicates that the distinct Mongol tribes of the day were at war with one another and were probably already engaged in a nomadic way of life. Around the twelfth century, another title appeared: *qan*, transcribed in English as Khan. Temujin was first elevated as Chinggis Khan by his own tribe in 1189, and was confirmed as such by all the Mongols in 1206, at a great gathering of Mongol nobles and high-ranking commanders of the Mongol cavalry on the Kerulen river. This gathering marked the unification of the Mongol tribes and the birth of the Mongol military machine, and was the first move toward the creation of a new order on the steppe.

Before Chinggis, the Mongols lacked a clear sense of their identity as a people. Chinggis's historic role was to endow them with such a sense. His strong identification with his ancestral homelands, almost akin to modern nationalism, is well illustrated by an incident that happened between him and three of his followers who had left him to join one of his Mongol rivals. He sent these people a message saying that they were now on their own, but that they should never let anyone other than a Mongol set up camp at the source of the three rivers, the Kerulen, the Tu'ula, and the Onon.

The Mongol tribes professed an ancestral shamanism; their great deity was the sky, which they worshipped together with the spirits inhabiting the sun, the moon, the stars, the mountains, the water, the trees and all natural things. As shamanists, they had no church, nor did they need one, since worship was effectively a matter of immediate communication between the individual and the world of nature. Indeed, the intermediacy of shaman priests was an option that Chinggis himself often preferred not to use. For shamanists, the soul is linked directly to Heaven and the individual is therefore the centre of his own universe. Heaven is our guide: under it we are born free and equal.

Chinggis Khan was never influenced by the passive philosophy of Buddhism and not at all by the rigid doctrines of Confucianism, which reduced the universe to the family or the state. The universe to which Chinggis and the Mongols owed allegiance was bound by neither kin nor place. That is why just two million Mongols, with 129,000 horsemen, could establish the largest land empire in world history. The other great peoples of Asia — for example, the Indians and the Chinese — were never able to match this achievement. The reason for this lies in their view of the world, which was more trammelled and restricted than that of the Mongols, who at the time lacked even a word for 'country'. (The word *ulus*, which in those days meant 'nation', has since acquired the additional meaning of 'country' in modern Mongolian.) And so the Mongols came to consider their tent as the universe.

The thirteenth-century Mongols represented pastoral civilisation, the nineteenth-century British, oceanic civilisation, and the twentieth-century Americans, scientific civilisation. What were the motives that led them to establish empires? The British and the Americans were seeking to colonise land and space: the Mongols were simply rising to the challenge. 'If Heaven grants a way,' Chinggis told his sons, 'you will embark on campaigns beyond the sea ... Beyond the mountain rocks you will launch campaigns ... Send back news on wings.'

The late Professor Owen Lattimore maintained that Chinggis Khan was the greatest strategist the world has ever produced. He wrote: 'As a military genius, able to take over new techniques and improve on them, Chinggis stands above Alexander the Great, Hannibal, Caesar, Attila and Napoleon.' The map on page xii shows the extent of the Mongol empire under Qubilai Khan compared with those of Alexander the Great and Napoleon. It stretched from Java and Korea in the east to Poland in the west, and from the Arctic Ocean in the north to Persia in the south. The Mongols opened a

THE MONGOL EMPIRE
compared with those of
ALEXANDER and NAPOLEON

Samarkand   Beijing

approx. 2,500 miles

•Moscow

•Paris

Rome

•Samarkand

•Baghdad

Cairo•

Ulaan-Baatar

Beijing

Hanoi

Empire of Alexander the Great 356–323 B.C. ·····
The Mongol Empire 1206–1368 ——
The Empire of Napoleon 1769–1821 - - -

transcontinental road between East and West, along which, for the first time in a thousand years, humans and cultural objects and influences could once again be safely exchanged. They linked Asia and Europe by horse relay stations which speeded up communications between the central places of the two continents. During the Mongols' Hungarian campaign in March 1242, news of the death of the Second Great Khan Ogodei took just forty days to get from the Mongol homeland to Budapest, some four thousand miles away. According to reports, urgent messages could be transmitted by express couriers at a rate of two hundred or more miles a day.

In the thirteenth century, the Mongol territories abutted the 'barbarian' Jin empire (1115–1234) to the south (including the region later known as Manchuria): China, under the Sung dynasty, lay beyond the Jin. The Jin people, originally nomads, had been heavily influenced by Chinese culture and had come to follow Confucian norms. To the south-west of Mongolia was the Xi Xia Kingdom of the Tangquts, and further west still, around the oases of Central Asia, were the Uighurs, a Turkish people once strong but now in military decline. By the early thirteenth century, fighting between the Jin and the Sung had seriously weakened both states. These troubles to the south, and a long period of relative internal peace, had diminished the pressure on the Mongols, who by the end of the twelfth century had significantly increased their livestock. To maintain their prosperity (and eventually transform themselves into a world power), they needed dynamic, centralised leadership of the sort that Chinggis Khan eventually provided.

Chinggis was a far-sighted ruler and a born diplomat, who understood the wishes of his people and led them skilfully. Between the start of his ascendancy and his death in 1227, not a single one of the generals with whom he built his empire had to be executed — not one of them betrayed him. (In this respect, empire-builders of the twentieth century would have done well to learn from him.) He established his empire and held it together with three vital ties: those of marriage (through skilful alliances), sworn brotherhood (a tie that only death could sever), and feudal patronage or friendship.

As a shamanist who lacked religious fervour and believed in the right to worship freely, between 1218 and 1222 Chinggis proclaimed to his subjects a policy of religious toleration. 'The Catholic inquisitors of Europe', wrote the historian Gibbon, '... might have been confounded by the example of a barbarian, who anticipated the lessons of philosophy and established by his laws a system of pure theism and perfect toleration.' This policy of toleration and respect for all religions, continued by Qubilai after his accession, was unique for its time. However, it was motivated less by high-mindedness than by expediency, for it was an effective weapon in Chinggis's wars against peoples of other religions (the Mongols were never popular, but people liked Chinggis's policy on religion), and it enabled Chinggis to manipulate the rivalries and conflicts between Muslims, Buddhists and Christians in the territories that he conquered.

Iron discipline and matchless speed were not the only reasons for the Mongols' success in their wars of conquest. It also owed much to their employment of foreign collaborators. (Eventually Turks outnumbered actual Mongols in the Mongol armies.) The Mongols under Chinggis and his successors showed little evidence of the xenophobia that has frequently resulted in the closing of China to outside influences. As a result of their flexible, pragmatic and receptive attitude, they learned much that was a source of great strength to them while establishing their empire and administering it.

In matters of punishment and reward, Chinggis was known to be strict, but also generous and fair. When the herdsmen Badai and Kishiliq informed him that Ong Khan was about to attack him, and thus saved his life and that of many of his men, he handed them the defeated Ong Khan's property, including his gold-painted tent.

Before Chinggis, the basic social and political unit of Mongol society was the patriarchal tribe, which focussed the loyalty of each individual. Chinggis broke up this tribal system, and replaced it with a feudal army organised according to an artificial decimal system, with units of between ten and ten thousand men, centred mainly on the thousands. Within these units, which covered Mongolia's entire manpower by means of universal conscription, he intermixed the tribes, especially those of his former enemies, which he broke up and distributed across the army. To lead the thousands, he appointed ninety-five elite commanders, chosen on the basis of merit; they included tribal chiefs, humble herdsmen like Badai and Kishiliq, and members of vassal clans. The resulting organisation had some features in common with the general staff of a modern army.

Under Chinggis in 1204, the Mongols adapted to their own use the Uighur script, which they employed to codify Mongol law, to diffuse the law among the Mongol tribes and to write this *History*. (Today this script, dropped by the Communists in favour of the Russian cyrillic alphabet, has been revived in what used to be the Mongolian People's Republic.)

There are four items of Mongol law that illustrate the character of Mongol society under Chinggis. Any person who eats in front of another without offering that person food should be executed. Anyone caught stealing anything of value may be freed after repaying nine times its worth. Anyone guilty of hurting a horse's eyes should be executed. And anyone found indulging in homosexual practices should be executed.

After securing his home front by uniting the Mongol tribes, Chinggis first subdued the steppe and desert nomads of Central Asia right up to the Dnieper river in southern Russia and only then turned south to attack the Jin, whom he considered a lesser danger as they were somewhat more sedentary. Peking (Beijing) fell to him in 1215, and by 1234, seven years after his death, the Jin empire lay in ruins. From here the Mongols vaulted south into China proper, where Qubilai established the Yuan dynasty in 1271 and finally overthrew the Sung in 1279.

The horsemanship of the Mongol cavalry is unrivalled in the history of war. Mongol archers conquered the world from their horses, wielding bows with a drawing strength of 166 pounds, accurate over six or seven hundred feet. Chinggis Khan, as Professor Lattimore said, was one of the world's greatest strategists. He kept his armies constantly on the move, for he feared that, left to themselves without an external enemy to unite them, they would start to fight among themselves. His campaigns were precisely planned and brilliantly executed. His generals were expert at siege warfare (which they learned from the Chinese and used to take walled fortresses), bridge building, and the lightning strike; and they were masters of the arts of deception, espionage, and psychological warfare. Field intelligence played a crucial part in Chinggis's wars, enabling him to mount flank attacks with flying horse columns, to encircle the enemy and block his escape, and to synchronise distant forces by signalling with smoke, lanterns and coloured flags.

By the time of his death, Chinggis had laid the foundations for a vast Eurasian empire that his immediate descendants extended to most of the known world, with the sea as their sole remaining barrier. (The Mongol fleet sent to subdue Japan was destroyed by the *kamikaze*, or divine wind, in 1281, and Mongol ships tried unsuccessfully to subdue Java.)

Reports by non-Mongols of the Mongol campaigns were

often grossly prejudiced and exaggerated. According to one, in 1225 the Mongols killed 1,600,000 people in a small city called Herat to the south-west of Samarkand; another puts the death toll even higher, at 2,400,000. But these reports can hardly be true, for at the time even Samarkand, capital of the territory, had a population of no more than 200,000. Another account, written in 1240 by Matthew Paris, a monk at St Albans near London, in his *Chronica Majora*, testifies to European dismay at reports of the Mongol horsemen then ravaging the settlements and cities of Russia. The Mongol horses were so huge, reported Paris, that they ate whole branches and even trees, and could only be mounted by means of three-step ladders. But these are histories written by the vanquished, just as our book is history written by the victors.

Chinggis Khan has become a byword in popular thinking for pitiless and wanton cruelty, but this picture of him is unfair, for his forces rarely used torture and he never once fought a war without first declaring it. Whether in their Russian or their Chinese campaigns, the Mongols under Chinggis always delivered a full warning to their intended victims: 'Give in within three or six days and we will spare you, otherwise we will fight you to the death and give no quarter.' They are generally credited with having kept their word.

As for the Mongol ponies, in truth they were rather small, but they were extremely tough, and made up in stamina and endurance for what they lacked in speed. They could gallop for thirty kilometres without pausing to rest.

The name Mongolia probably derives from Onongol, meaning 'Boy River'. Mongolia is a land of clear blue skies, treeless green pasture, and, to the south, stony desert. It is cold, dry, and windy for most of the year, but a paradise on earth in July and August. On a hot summer day, sitting among the desert stones and watching the wonderful array of mirages rise before you from the sand or shimmer in the distance like sheets of water, you are overcome by a delight beyond words. The stars seem close enough to touch to those sitting silently

on the sand at night, soothed into a state of tranquil clarity
by the chirping of cicadas.

> The stars smile down at you,
> the cicadas lull you into sleep;
> now and then the land of khans
> changes its guard.
> As the mirages rise before your eyes
> you forget your age.
> The land of the camel
> moves forwards and backwards.*

This book, known to Mongols as the *Tobchi'an* or 'History',
has appeared under a variety of names, including *The Secret
History of the Mongols, The Life of Chinggis Khan, The Real
Record of Chinggis Khan,* and *The Secret History of the Yuan
Dynasty.* It has been translated into many languages, including
English, Japanese, French, German, Chinese, Russian, Hungarian, and Polish. Like Chinggis himself, the book is highly
controversial. We cannot be sure when it was written or who
wrote it. I myself have argued that it was written in 1228, but
other scholars date it at 1240 or 1324. Whatever the case, the
book is unique as the only near-contemporary account of the
life of Chinggis Khan.

In 1990, I translated into English the 1980 edition of the
History, collated by Eldengtei and Oyuundalai for the Inner
Mongolian People's Press. Mine was the third English translation after those by Igor de Rachewiltz (published in serial
form as *The Secret History of the Mongols* by the Australian
National University between 1971 and 1984) and Francis
Woodman Cleaves (published under the same title by Harvard
University Press in 1982). This, then, is the fourth English-
language version of the *History,* recast by Sue Bradbury,
editorial director of The Folio Society, for the general reader
from my 1990 translation, and entitled *The Golden History
of the Mongols.* Another Mongol book published in the

---

* Poem by Urgunge Onon. Ed.

seventeenth century bore this same title, but I still think it a right name for the present edition, for in the thirteenth century Chinggis Khan and his family were called 'golden' in much the same way as the kings and queens of England are called royal. 'The night-guards are there . . . to guard my golden life,' said Chinggis. And around 1223 Chinggis said (in two lines recorded in a poem):

> Should my golden body weaken,
> so be it.
> But my existing dynasty
> must not be broken up.*

URGUNGE ONON
Mongolia and Inner Asia Studies Unit
University of Cambridge

EDITOR'S NOTE

There are inconsistencies within the text, especially with regard to names and family relationships. Where confusions arise these have been either corrected or explained in footnotes, but the text remains substantially faithful to the original, inconsistencies included.

* For the Mongol text, see overleaf.

SOURCES

1 *The Study of the Mongol Art of War: The Strategy of Chinggis Khan* by Dalantai, Military Science Publishing House, Chen-De, China, 1990.

2 *The History and the Life of Chinggis Khan* (The Secret History of the Mongols) tr. by Urgunge Onon, E. J. Brill, Leiden, 1990.

3 *The Mongols' Campaign in Europe* by Shinobu Iwamura, San-Sei-Do, Tokyo, 1941.

4 *The Rise of Chinggis Khan and His Conquest of North China* by Desmond Martin, The Johns Hopkins Press, Baltimore, 1950.

5 *Genghis Khan Conqueror of the World* by Leo de Hartog, I. B. Tauris & Co. Ltd, 1989.

6 *The Mongols and Russia* by George Vernadsky, Yale University Press, New Haven and Oxford University Press, 1953.

ᠪᠢ ᠴᠢᠮᠠᠢᠢ ᠬᠠᠢᠢᠷᠠᠯᠠᠨᠠ᠃

ᠾ ᠴᠢᠮᠠᠢᠢ ᠰᠠᠨᠠᠵᠤ ᠨᠢᠳᠦ ᠳᠡᠭᠡᠨ ᠨᠢᠯᠪᠤᠰᠤ ᠲᠠᠢ ᠢᠠᠪᠠᠨ᠎ᠠ᠃ ᠿ

CHAPTER ONE
The origins of the Mongol clans and the birth of Temujin.

WHEN CHINGGIS KHAN WAS BORN, HIS DESTINY HAD ALREADY BEEN ORDAINED BY HEAVEN above. He was descended from Borte Chino, whose name means Wolf, and Qo'ai Maral, whose name means Beautiful Doe. They had crossed the lake together and settled by the Onon river at Burqan-qaldun — the Place of the Cliff. There, their son Batachi Khan was born.

And the son of Batachi Khan was Tamacha; and the son of Tamacha was Qorichar-mergen (which means Wise Hunter); and the son of Qorichar-mergen was A'ujam-boro'ul; and the son of A'ujam-boro'ul was Sali-qacha'u; and the son of Sali-qacha'u was Yeke-nidun; and the son of Yeke-nidun the Wide-Eyed was Sem-sochi; and the son of Sem-sochi was Qarchu.

Qarchu's son, Borjigidai-mergen, married Mongqoljin, the fairest of the Mongols, while Borjigidai's son, Toroqoljin the Rich, had a wife called Boroqchin-qo'a, a young servant called Boroldai-suyalbi, two fine geldings — the Great One and the Grey One — and two strapping sons — Duwa-soqor and Dobun-mergen.

Duwa-soqor had only one eye, in the middle of his forehead, but he could see as far as three days' journey* with it.

One day, with his younger brother, Duwa-soqor climbed the rocky precipice of Burqan-qaldun, and looking down from its height he saw a mass of people moving slowly downstream, along the winding Tunggelik river.

'They have struck camp,' he said, 'and they're coming this way. There's a black-covered waggon, with a most beautiful girl sitting up on the front seat. If she doesn't already belong to anyone, you shall have her, brother. Let's go and ask.' And he sent young Dobun-mergen to take a closer look.

---

* One 'journey' was about ten miles, the distance that could be covered by a whole camp in one day.

When Dobun-mergen approached he found that she was indeed truly beautiful, and of good reputation. Her name, Alan-qo'a, was well-known in the region, and she had not yet been promised to any man.

Her mother, Barqujin-qo'a, was the daughter of Barqudai-mergen, Lord of the Kol Barqujin valley. She had been married to the Lord of the Qori-tumed, Qorilartai-mergen, and had given birth to Alan-qo'a down by the Clean river.

But Qorilartai quarrelled with his people when they banned the hunting of sable, squirrel and other wild animals in the land of the Qori-tumed; and he and his clan decided to move on to the Burqan-qaldun — a land rich in wild creatures and gazelles. There, by the Sacred mountain, they made contact with the gods and spirit lords of the place, and it was as they were approaching Uriangqai that Dobun-mergen met them and begged Alan-qo'a's hand in marriage. She went on to bear him two sons, Bugunutei and Belgunutei.

Meanwhile his elder brother Duwa-soqor also had sons — four of them — but he died soon afterwards, and his sons despised their uncle Dobun-mergen and refused to take him into the family. Instead they moved away and established four separate clans which became known as the Four Peoples.

One day Dobun-mergen went hunting on Toqochaq peak, and there in the forest he met a man of the Urianqad who had killed a three-year-old deer, and was roasting its ribs and bowels.

'My friend,' said Dobun-mergen, 'give me some meat from your roasting-spit.'

'With pleasure,' said the hunter. And, keeping only the lungs, head and skin of the beast (in which the spirit was), he gave the rest of the meat to Dobun-mergen.

Dobun-mergen loaded up the deer on his horse and went on his way. And on the road he met a poor man leading a little boy by the hand.

'Who are you?' asked Dobun-mergen, and the man answered: 'I'm from the Ma'aliq Bayya'ud. I'm starving to death. I'd give this son of mine for a hunk of that beast's flesh.'

With that, Dobun-mergen tore the hind leg off the deer and gave it to him. Then he took the boy home with him as his servant.

Not long afterwards Dobun-mergen died; but Alan-qo'a bore three more sons despite the loss of her husband. Their names were Buqu-qadagi, Buqatu-salji and Bodonchar-mungqaq, which means Bodonchar the fool.

Then Belgunutei and Bugunutei began to whisper about their mother behind her back. 'This mother of ours', they said, 'has borne three sons without a husband. What's more, she has not been passed on to our father's brothers or cousins. The only man in the house is from the Ma'aliq Bayya'ud: those three boys must be his.'

But Alan-q'oa sensed what they were saying about her. One spring day she boiled some mutton and sat all five boys down in a row. Then she gave them each an arrow, saying: 'Break it!'

They all broke the arrows easily and tossed them aside. Then she took five arrows and bound them together. She gave the arrows to each boy in turn, saying: 'Break them!' But however hard they tried, the clutch of arrows would not break.

Then Alan-qo'a said to Belgunutei and Bugunutei: 'My sons, I know you have had your suspicions. I know you've been talking behind my back, saying: "Where did these three boys come from, whose sons are they?" Well, it's natural you should ask.

'Every night a shining yellow man slipped into the tent through the light of the smoke hole and the gap at the top of the door. He caressed my belly and his light seemed to sink into me. When he went out it was as though he slunk like a yellow dog between the light of sun and moon.

> Why do you whisper such nonsense?
> Why can you not understand?
> My sons are the children of Heaven
> born to be lords of the land.
> With the ranks of the black-haired, the hatless,
> these boys you try to compare,

why do you not recognise them —
my sons, who are lords of the air?'

Then Alan-qo'a went on to instruct her five sons with the
following words: 'You boys were all born of my flesh. If you
stand alone you can easily be broken, just as those five arrow-
shafts were broken. But if you stand together, like this bundle
of shafts, no one can ever overcome you.'

Not long afterwards their mother was no more, and after
her death the brothers divided up the property and the livestock between them. Belgunutei, Bugunutei, Buqu-qatagi and
Buqatu-salji all took a share, but they decided that Bodonchar-
mungqaq was too stupid and dull to merit anything, so they
left him out of the reckoning.

When he found he was no longer regarded as one of the
family, Bodonchar thought: 'What am I doing here? Why
have I stayed so long?' And he rode away on an off-white,
draggle-tailed, sure-footed nag with sores on its black-striped
back. 'If I'm to die, let me die,' he said. 'If I'm to live, let me
live.' And he went down to the Onon river where he built
himself a grass yurt on the island of Baljun.

There he settled, and one day he saw a young female
hawk as it caught and ate a black pheasant. So he captured
the hawk, using the tail hairs of his off-white, draggle-tailed,
sore-backed, black-striped nag as a snare, and he tamed and
reared it.

When he was hungry he sought out the wild beasts that the
wolves had cornered at the base of the cliffs, and shot them,
sharing the meat with his hawk. Or sometimes he picked up
the wolves' leftovers and ate them. Thus he fed himself and
his hawk as the year passed.

Spring came, and with it the arrival of the duck. Bodonchar
starved his hawk, and then set it at them. He hung his catch
of ducks and geese on the trees until

from every withered branch
arose a stench,
an odour dark and rank
from every shrivelled trunk.

Meanwhile a group of travellers had moved camp from the sunless side of Mount Duyiren, down to the Tunggelik stream. After flying his hawk, Bodonchar used to visit them, drinking kumiss* with them during the day, and going back to his own yurt to sleep.

Some of the men wanted Bodonchar's hawk, but he did not give it to them. They didn't seem interested in his tribe or his family, and he, for his part, asked them no questions. Yet he kept coming and going.

One day Bodonchar's elder brother, Buqu-qatagi, thinking that he had gone downstream along the Onon river, came to look for him. He found the camp and asked the people there whether they had come across a man with a curious-looking horse.

They replied: 'There's a man with a horse like that who comes here every day. He has a hawk with him. He drinks our kumiss, and then goes away. We don't know where he spends the night. When the wind is in the north-east, the feathers and down from the geese and ducks killed by his hawk blow tumbling down here like snow. He can't be far away. Why don't you wait for him? It's time he was here.'

Not long after a man rode slowly upstream. It was Bodonchar. When Buqu-qatagi saw him he recognised him instantly, and led him off up the Onon river.

Bodonchar, jogging along behind his elder brother, observed after a while: 'A body needs a head, and a cape needs a collar.' His brother made no answer, so he said the same words again, and still his brother remained silent. They travelled a little further, and Bodonchar repeated his words for a third time.

'What are you getting at?' asked Buqu-qatagi presently. To which Bodonchar replied: 'Those people down by the Tunggelik stream, they have no high or low, good or bad, great or small, head or hoof. Everyone is equal. They are simple people. Why don't we plunder them?'

'Well,' said his elder brother, 'if you're right we should talk to the others when we get back to the yurt and make a plan.'

So on their return the brothers made a plan, and then set out

* Kumiss is fermented mares' milk.

on horseback. Bodonchar himself was sent galloping ahead as a scout, and on the way he took a prisoner — a woman, four or five months pregnant. He asked her who she was.

'I am of the Jarchi'ut tribe,' she said. 'I come from the Greater Uriangqai.'

Then the brothers fell upon the camp, and with their plunder — livestock, property and the people themselves as servants and slaves — they settled down to a new life.

The pregnant woman stayed with Bodonchar and bore a son. They called him Jajiradai, because he was the son of a foreigner, and he, and his son, and his son's son, became the fathers of the Jadaran clan.

The woman also bore Bodonchar's son, and because she was a captive they called him Ba'aridai. He, and his son, and his son's many sons, were the fathers of the Menen-Ba'arin clan.

And from Belgunutei was descended the Belgunut clan; from Bugunutei, the Bugunut clan; from Buqu-qatagi, the Qatagin clan; from Buqatu-salji, the Salji'ut clan; and from Bodonchar, the Borjigin clan.

Bodonchar then had a son by his principal wife, the one who had been promised to him in childhood, and he had another by a concubine who had come to him as part of his wife's mother's dowry.* This last was called Jewuredei, and even though he was a concubine's son and could not inherit from his father, he was, at first, allowed to take part in the ceremony of the Jugeli. Here the skin, head and hooves of an ox, horse or sheep are stretched on a pole as an offering to the family ancestors.

But after Bodonchar's death, the family noticed that a man from the Greater Uriangqai was constantly to be seen coming and going from Jewuredei's tent, so they banished him from the Jugeli ceremony and told him to set up his own clan. Thus Jewuredei became the father of the Jeured.

---

* Three types of dowry were customary during the period covered by the *History* — that which remained under the bride's jurisdiction (including housemaids, livestock and valuables); that which was given to the groom by the bride's parents (over which the bride had no rights); and the items of clothing given by the bride to the groom's parents on first meeting.

Qabichi-ba'atur's* son was called Menen-tuden—the Great Chief—and he in his turn had seven sons—Qachi-kuluk, Qachin, Qachi'u, Qachula, Qachi'un, Qaraldai and Nachin-ba'atur.

Qachi-kuluk had a son, Qaidu, born to Mother Nomolun, while Qachin's son was given the name Noyagidai, because of his lordly and overbearing temperament. From him the Noyakin clan was descended. Qachi'u's son was called Baru-latai because he had a clumsy body and crude table manners—from him the Barulas clan was descended. Qachula's sons had vulgar eating habits too, so they were called Big Barula and Small Barula, and they were the fathers of all the other Barulas clans.

There was no leader among Qaraldai's sons—they stirred the porridge together and formed the Buda'at clan. Qachi'un's son was called Adarkidai: he was thoroughly obstinate in his dealings with his brothers and sisters, and broke away to form the Adargin clan.

So from all these sons were descended the clans of the Uru'ut and the Mangqut; the Tayyichi'ut, Besut, Oronar, Qongqotan and Arulat clans, and the clans of Sonit, Qab-turqas and Geniges.

And over them all ruled Qabul Khan, Lord of all the Mon-gols. And after him, Ambaqai Khan, the son of Senggum-bilqe, who was specially chosen by Qabul Khan even though he had seven sons of his own.

Then Ambaqai Khan promised his daughter in marriage to a Tatar people who lived on the river Urshi'un, between the Bayur and Kolen lakes. And while he was escorting her there, he was captured by the Juyin Tatars—the frontier army of the Jins—and dragged before the Altan Khan of the Kitad.

Using a Besutei man, Balaqachi, as a messenger, he managed to get a message out to Qabul Khan's son Qutula, and to one of his own ten sons. The message was:

'I who am Khan of all, and Lord of all Nations, have been taken prisoner by the Tatars while escorting my own daughter to her wedding. Do not trust as I have trusted. Vow vengeance

---

* *ba'atur*: hero.

on mine enemies until your fingernails splinter and your ten
fingers rot.'

Meanwhile Yisugei-ba'atur was flying hawks down by the
Onon river when he ran into Yeke-chiledu of the Merkit, who
was taking his new wife home. Craning his neck for a closer
look, Yisugei saw a woman whose complexion was of un-
paralleled beauty. He galloped swiftly back to his yurt and
fetched his brothers, and together they returned, intent on
capture.

When Chiledu saw them he was afraid. He whacked his
dun horse on the rump, and galloped back round the hill to
where his wife — the Lady Ho'elun — was waiting in their
cart. By then the brothers were close behind him.

'Did you see their faces?' asked Ho'elun urgently. 'They're
after your life. There will be girls wherever you go — un-
married ones, sitting up on the front seat of their waggons,
married ones hidden away from prying eyes. As long as you're
alive you have a chance of finding another woman to love.
Perhaps you will call her Ho'elun. Oh, save your life, Chiledu,
and as long as you live remember the kiss and the smell of
me!'

And so saying she took off her shirt, and thrust it towards
him. Even as he bent forward to take it, the three men came
round the spur of the hill, and Chiledu clapped his whip to
his horse's rump, and fled upstream along the Onon river.

They pursued him over seven hills before they came back
to where Ho'elun sat in the waggon. Then Yisugei-ba'atur
took the leading rein while his elder brother went ahead and
the younger walked beside the shafts. As they went their way,
Lady Ho'elun said: 'My husband Chiledu,

> in the rough wind
> his hair has never blown,
> in the wild land
> his belly has never hungered...

What will become of him?' And as she rocked to and fro her
plaits swung in a frenzy against her breasts and her back.
'What will become of me?' she cried aloud, and the Onon

river churned and the forest echoed to the sound of her weeping.

As he walked along beside the shafts the younger brother said:

> 'The man you embraced
> has crossed many ridges,
> the man for whom you cry
> has forded many rivers.
> However hard you weep
> from however far away,
> he will not see you,
> and should you search for him
> you will not find the way.

Calm down,' he advised.

Then Yisugei took Lady Ho'elun into his yurt and that is the story of her capture.

As Ambaqai Khan had sent messages both to Qada'an and Qutula, the Mongol and Tayyichi'ut clans gathered together in the Qorqonaq forest beside the Onon river. There they made Qutula their khan, and there was much dancing and feasting in celebration. They danced round the Many-Leaved Tree of Qorqonaq for so long that the dust came up to their knees and they wore a trench in the earth almost to their chests.

As soon as he became khan, Qutula rode out against the Tatars to avenge Ambaqai. Thirteen times he fought with Koton-baraqa and Jali-buqa, and thirteen times he was defeated.

In the meantime Yisugei-ba'atur was making raids on Temujin-uge, Qori-buga and other Tatar chieftains, and when he got back he found to his delight that Lady Ho'elun was pregnant. They were camped at Deli'un-boldaq on the Onon river at the time, and that was where Chinggis Khan was born. They gave him the name of his father's defeated enemy, Temujin, and he was born holding a clot of blood in his hand as big as a knucklebone.

Lady Ho'elun went on to have four sons — Temujin, Qasar,

Qachi'un and Temuge — and a daughter, Temulun. Temujin
was nine when his sister was born, and it was then that his
father decided to find him a wife from among his mother's
relations. Father and son set out together, and between Chek-
char and Chiqurgu they met Dei-sechen, the Wise Uncle of
the Onggirat tribe.

Dei-sechen greeted them, asking: 'Where are you going?'

Yisugei replied: 'I'm taking this boy of mine to the Olqunu'ut clan to see if his mother's brothers can provide him with
a wife.'

Then Dei-sechen said: 'That boy has fire in his eyes, and
his face burns bright. Listen, Yisugei, I had a dream last night.
I dreamed that a white falcon flew down out of the sky
clasping the sun and moon in its claws, and landed on my
hand. I talked to the others about it: we could look up at the
sun and the moon, but we couldn't get near them. Yet a white
gerfalcon brought them within my grasp. What did it mean?
Yisugei, it was a good dream: it showed your coming and that
of your son. What else could it have been but a good omen
for our people?

'From time immemorial the Onggirat have

> taken the colour of our sisters' children,
> taken the colour of our daughters' faces.

Our clan cannot compete:

> we give instead our daughters to the khans,
> our fair-faced daughters riding high on waggons
> drawn by camels,
> sent off at the trot,
> until they take their places on a throne.

Our clan cannot compete:

> instead we set our fair-faced daughters up,
> each daughter on the front seat of a waggon
> drawn by a camel,
> black or darkly grey . . .
> We send her off until at last she sits
> upon a throne beside one of your own,

a lady fit for a lord...

Of old the Onggirat have been shielded by women:

> we have made our daughters queens,
> those queens have pleaded for us,
> their complexions answered for us,
> and we have hidden behind
> the faces of our sisters' children.
> Our sons are renowned for their camping grounds,
> our daughters for the fairness of their faces.

Come to my tent, Yisugei. My daughter is young. You should look at her.'

And Dei-sechen led them, the man and the boy, to his yurt and bade them dismount.

When Yisugei saw Dei-sechen's daughter, he was entranced by the light in her face, the fire in her eyes. She was ten years old — a year older than Temujin — and her name was Borte. She lingered in Yisugei's thoughts all night, and the following day he went to Dei-sechen and asked that he might have her for his son.

Then Dei-sechen said: 'If many men had asked for my daughter's hand, and I had finally given her away, I should have earned the respect of all my kin. If I give her away to the first who asks for her, I shall forfeit that respect. But I don't want a daughter of mine to grow old on her own doorstep, and I want you to have my daughter for your son. Leave him here as my son-in-law and go your way.'

And so they were agreed.

Yisugei-ba'atur said: 'I leave you my son to be your son-in-law. Be warned: he has a terrible fear of dogs.* Keep him away from them.'

And giving Dei-sechen his spare horse as a present, Yisugei said farewell to his son and departed.

At Chekcher in the Yellow steppe country he came across some Tatars who were feasting. By this time he was thirsty,

---

* In fact there is no further mention of this fear in the *History*. It may be a reference — well founded as it turns out — to Yisugei's enemies (see below).

so he rode up to them, hoping for food and drink. But the Tatars recognised him.

'It is Yisugei-kiyan,' they whispered, remembering how he had robbed and insulted them in the past. So they mixed poison into the food they offered him, and on his way home he was violently sick. By the time he reached his yurt Yisugei was very ill, and after three days it seemed clear that he would die.

In the year 1110 Yisugei said: 'I am going to die. Is anyone near me?'

'I am here,' said Monglik, Charaqa's son.

Yisugei called him close. 'Monglik, my boy,' said he, 'I have children of my own. I left Temujin with his new bride only a few days ago, and it was on my way home that the Tatars took their revenge on me. Now I am dying. I beg you to look after my little ones for me — your brothers, your widowed sister-in-law. And fetch my son home, Monglik. Quickly.'

With that Yisugei died.

'The old woman, Qo'aqchin, hid Lady Borte
in a black-covered wagon' (*page 25*)

Chinggis Khan with his friends in the snow:
'"If a meeting has been agreed neither snow nor rain should
impede you or make you late"' (*page 32*)

CHAPTER TWO
His childhood and youth. His marriage and the kidnapping of his wife, Lady Borte.

MONGLIK DID NOT STAY TO ASK QUESTIONS, BUT WENT IMMEDIATELY TO DEI-SECHEN. 'My master is missing Temujin,' he said. 'His heart aches. I must take his son back to him.'

Dei-sechen answered: 'If the *quda** is missing his son, he shall have him back. But let him return to me before long.'

So Monglik took Temujin home.

That spring Orbei and Soqatai, the wives of Ambaqai Khan, went up to the land where their ancestors lay buried. As was customary, they dressed as daughters-in-law, and they went without waiting for Lady Ho'elun. When she caught up with them she upbraided them:

'Do you think you can keep me from my share of the sacrificial meat and drink, our ancestors' offerings, just because my husband is dead and my children as yet unfledged? I see you eat before me shamelessly. You would have left me asleep and gone without me.'

Then the wives of Ambaqai Khan answered her, saying:

'Who says that because we called you, we should feed you too?

> If you find food
> you eat it.

Who says that because we invited you, we should feed you too?

> If food is given to you
> you eat it.

* *quda*: a relation by marriage or marriage contract.

Did you think Ambaqai was dead too? Is that why even you, Ho'elun, speak against us? We must find a way of leaving these mothers and children behind,' said they, 'we don't want to take them with us.'

And the next day a group of the Tayyichi'ut tribe, led by Tarqutai and Todo'en-girte, set off down the Onon river, leaving Lady Ho'elun and the other mothers and children behind. When Charaqa, Monglik's father, chided them, Todo'en-girte simply said:

> 'The deep water has dried up,
> the shining stone is worn away.
> It is over.'

And as they moved off they taunted the old man, saying: 'Who do you think you are, telling us what to do?' Then they struck him in the back with a spear.

Wounded, Charaqa came back to his yurt, and, as he lay there in dreadful pain, Temujin came to him. Charaqa said: 'All the people your good father gathered together have been tempted away by the Tayyichi'ut. When I chided them, this was my reward.'

Then Temujin wept and left the yurt, and Lady Ho'elun herself set off on horseback, carrying the clan flag, and managed to persuade half the people to return. Even then they wouldn't stay, but soon set off again in search of the Tayyichi'ut brothers. So Lady Ho'elun, the other mothers and their children were left in the camp.

> Lady Ho'elun, a woman of wisdom,
> brought up her little ones, nurtured her children,
> wore her hat tall and tied it up tightly,
> hoisted her skirts up, sashing them bravely,
> running upstream on the banks of the Onon,
> gathering wild pears, fruits of the region,
> nourishing the bellies and throats of her children.
> Born into pain was the lady, their mother,
> reared into fortune her fortunate children.
> Taking a pointed stick of the juniper,
> digging up roots to nourish her children,

> she fed them with onions, fed them with garlic,
> saw how the sons of her belly could flourish,
> reared them to rule by her noble example.
> Thus on a diet of seeds they were nourished
> and as wise men and lawgivers they flourished.
> Thus on wild leeks and wild garlic were reared
> the marvellous sons of a marvellous mother.
> Powerful, straight and courageous they grew,
> and, stalking together, said: 'We can help too.'
> With rods, lines and hooks on the banks of the
>   Onon
> they fished for the crookedest fish in the river,
> with needles as fishhooks they took scad and
>   salmon,
> with different nets they scooped up small fishes,
> and, helping their mother, they grew and were
>   grateful.

One day when Temujin was fishing with his brothers, Qasar, Bekter and Belgutei, they caught a bright minnow. Bekter and Belgutei immediately snatched it away, at which Temujin and Qasar went back to the yurt and told their mother, saying: 'A bright minnow took our hook, but Bekter and Belgutei snatched our fish away from us.'

Then their noble mother said: 'You are always quarrelling, the younger ones with the elder. Why? You know the saying:

> Apart from our shadows we have no friends,
> Apart from our tails we have no meat.*

Who is going to look after us if we don't look after ourselves? You should be thinking about how to avenge yourselves on the Tayyichi'ut people. Instead you squabble like Old Mother Alan's son in the story. You should learn to pull together.'

Temujin and Qasar were not so easily satisfied. They said: 'Only yesterday we shot down a lark with a horn-tipped

---

* Mongolian sheep store thick deposits of fat on their tails, off which they feed (like a camel off his hump), and which serve as a food source for the Mongolians.

arrow, and they took that away too. How can we be friends when they do things like that?'

Throwing open the door, they went out.

There was Bekter, sitting on top of a small hill, minding the horses — a herd of pale bay geldings. Temujin crept up behind him and Qasar worked his way round to the front, but just as they were taking aim with their bows, Bekter saw them and said:

'We are still smarting from our defeat at the hands of the Tayyichi'ut, and asking ourselves over and over again who should settle the score. You shouldn't let someone like me be the dirt in your mouth, the fishbone in your throat. At a time like this,

> apart from our shadows we have no friends,
> apart from our tails we have no meat.

Don't treat me like this; don't put out the fire in my hearth. Don't leave Belgutei lonely!'

Then, having spoken, he sat cross-legged and waited. Without a word Temujin and Qasar came on, one from behind, the other from in front, and when they were within range they shot Bekter and left his body where it fell.

When they returned to the yurt their noble mother saw what they had done written in their faces:

'You destroyers,' she said:

> You two came out of my womb by accident:
> you, with a black blood clot in your hand,
> like a dog gnawing on its afterbirth,
> like a panther ravening among the rocks,
> like a lion raging out of control,
> like a monster swallowing its prey alive,
> like a falcon harrying its own shadow,
> like a pike's indifferent and silent maw,
> like a camel chewing the heel of its foal,
> like a jackal defending the mouth of its den,
> like a tiger hunting for the sake of hunting
> or a wild dog attacking without need,
> thus you have killed!

> Apart from our shadows we have no friends,
> apart from our tails, we have no meat.

At such a time! When our hatred should be directed at the Tayyichi'ut, and we are asking ourselves who shall be our champion and how we shall live, you two are revenging yourselves on each other!'

And with much citing of old sayings and much quoting of the wisdom of the sages, she berated her sons for their foolish cruelty.

Not long afterwards, Tarqutai-kiriltuq of the Tayyichi'ut clan came to the camp with an armed guard and said:

> 'The lambs are shedding their fleece,
> the sheep are growing up.'

By this he meant that it had not escaped the clan's notice that Temujin and his brothers were now nearly men.

Ho'elun was frightened and took the hint. She and her sons built a stockade in the thickest part of the forest. Even as Belgutei tore down the trees and hauled them into place, Qasar was keeping the enemy at bay by countering their fire, while the three younger children — Qachi'un, Temuge and Temulun — slipped into the safety of a narrow gorge. As the struggle continued the Tayyichi'ut clan shouted out:

'It's Temujin we're interested in. Send him out, and we won't bother the rest of you.'

When they heard this they quickly mounted Temujin on a horse and covered his escape. As he fled through the forest the Tayyichi'ut saw him and set off in hot pursuit. But he plunged into a thicket on the Tergune heights, and, as it was too thick for them to penetrate, they surrounded it and bided their time.

Temujin spent three nights in the thicket before he dared move. On the fourth night he cautiously led his horse towards the opening, but the saddle-straps and breast-straps worked loose, and he found that his saddle had fallen off somewhere behind him.

'The saddle-strap I can understand,' said Temujin to himself, 'but why should the breast-strap have come loose?

Perhaps it's a sign from Heaven. I'd better go back.'

So he turned round and spent another three nights in the thicket.

Again on the fourth night he moved off cautiously towards the entrance, but this time a white rock, the size of a tent, fell and blocked the opening.

'Could this be a sign from Heaven too?' he asked himself; and, turning back, he spent a further three nights in the thicket.

Finally, after nine nights without food, he said to himself: 'Anything is better than dying here without a name. I will go out.'

The opening was still blocked by the white rock the size of a tent, but he cut through the trees at the side with the knife he carried for making arrows, and pushed his horse through.

As soon as he emerged the Tayyichi'ut, who had been standing guard, pounced on him and led him away a prisoner.

After the capture of Temujin, Tarqutai-kiriltuq went to his people and ordered them to let him stay for one night at each of their camps in turn. On Red Circle Day,* which is the sixteenth day of the first month of summer and the day when the pasture begins to grow afresh, the Tayyichi'ut sat down to feast until sunset on the banks of the Onon river. They took Temujin with them, but as luck would have it he was put in charge of a feeble young man, and, as the crowd broke up after the feast and the people began to make their way home, Temujin seized his chance. He jerked the rope attached to his wooden halter away from the boy, struck him on the head with it, and ran.

'If I lie down in the forest,' he thought, 'I'll soon be spotted.'

So, taking advantage of the wooden collar, or *cangue*, which had been used to fetter him, he launched himself down the torrential river, using the *cangue* as a pillow to keep his head above water.

In no time at all the feeble guard had raised the alarm.

* 'Red Circle Days' occurred on the sixteenth day of each lunar month, when it was thought that the sun and moon were facing each other. The night preceding a Red Circle Day was known as 'Circle Moon' or 'Full Moon'.

'I've lost the hostage,' he cried in a loud voice. And all the people came back and searched the Onon forest, for the moon was up and it was like day.

It so happened that Sorqan-shira of the Suldus was just passing by and he spotted Temujin lying in the torrent.

'So,' he said to Temujin, 'this is the kind of cleverness that makes men say of you: "There is a fire in his eyes and a light in his face." This is why you have roused the envy of your Tayyichi'ut kinsmen. Well, you just go on lying there. I won't tell.'

And having said this, he went away.

Meanwhile the Tayyichi'ut were saying to each other: 'We'd better go back and search again'; so when he caught up with them, Sorqan-shira said: 'Why don't we go back along exactly the same paths and look for the places we might have missed? Then we'll meet here again.'

They all agreed and set off, going back along exactly the same paths and searching as they went. Once more Sorqan-shira passed the place where Temujin was hiding and said:

'Your kinsmen are approaching: they are sharpening their mouths and their teeth. Lie still and keep your courage up.'

Then, when he heard them saying to each other: 'We'd better go back and search again', Sorqan-shira said: 'You Tayyichi'ut noblemen have lost a man in broad daylight, how can you hope to find him again at night? Why don't we go back down the same paths as before and make sure we haven't missed a single hiding place? If we can't find him this time, we'll call off the search until tomorrow morning. After all, a man in a wooden halter can't get very far!'

They agreed and resumed the search, and as they went their way Sorqan-shira slipped down to where Temujin lay and said: 'We have agreed to have one more look. If we fail to find you, we'll come back tomorrow. Wait until you see us going home, then try to find your mother and younger brothers! If anyone sees you, don't tell them about our meeting.'

And with that he disappeared.

When the Tayyichi'ut had given up the search and gone

away, Temujin thought to himself: 'I was forced to stay over-
night in each camp in turn, and yesterday, when I stayed in
Sorqan-shira's yurt, I could tell that his two sons were sorry
for me. After all, they loosened my *cangue* so that I could
sleep more comfortably. Just now Sorqan-shira found me
hiding, but he chose not to give me away. Perhaps he will save
me.'

So Temujin started off down the Onon river to look for
Sorqan-shira's yurt.

It was outside Sorqan-shira's tent that the mares' milk was
churned all through the night, so it was not difficult to find
the right place. 'I'll hear the churning before I reach the yurt,'
Temujin said to himself, and indeed he did. He presented
himself to Sorqan-shira, who said: 'Didn't I tell you to go and
look for your mother and brothers? Why have you come to
me?'

But his two sons, Chimba and Chila'un, spoke up and said:
'When a sparrow wants to hide from a hawk where does it
fly? Into a bush. Temujin has done the same. How can you
be angry with him?'

They disapproved of their father's words, and, freeing
Temujin from his halter, they burned it on the fire. Then they
hid him in a cart full of sheeps' wool at the back of the yurt,
instructing their younger sister, Qada'an,* to take care of him
and not to breathe a word to a living soul.

By the third day the Tayyichi'ut were getting suspicious.
'Perhaps one of us has hidden him,' they said. 'We'd better
search all the yurts.'

When they got to Sorqan-shira's yurt they even looked
under the bed, and when they got to the cart they began
to pull the wool away from the place where Temujin was
crouching. They were on the point of uncovering his foot
when Sorqan-shira said: 'How could anyone bury themselves
in wool in this heat?' and the searchers climbed down and
went away.

* Qada'an later became one of Chinggis Khan's wives: she was
Queen of the 'Fourth Palace', i.e. the camp he established at Baljuna
lake.

After they had gone Sorqan-shira said: 'You nearly had me blowing in the wind like ashes that time. Now off you go and find your mother and your younger brothers.'

He gave Temujin a white-mouthed, tawny mare that was barren, cooked him a fatted lamb, and prepared one small leather bag and another large one, full of kumiss. He did not give him a saddle or tinder pouch, but found him a bow and two arrows.* Then he sent him away.

Temujin set out, and eventually he arrived at the place where his mother and brothers had built the stockade. Then, following tracks in the grass, he went upstream along the Onon river and came to the point where the Kimurqa stream joins it from the west. Pursuing the course of the Kimurqa far upstream, he finally came upon his family, who were living on the Qorchukui hill on the Beder spur, overlooking the stream.

United again, mother and sons found themselves a camp site by the Koko lake on Black Heart mountain.† Called the Blue lake, it opens out of the Senggur river which rises in the Gurelgu mountains on the southern side of Burqan-qaldun. There they stayed, living on marmots and field-mice.

One day thieves stole up to the yurt, and, before anyone could stop them, disappeared, taking eight bay geldings with them. Without a horse between them, the brothers could only look on and wait for the return of Belgutei with their one remaining horse — a bald-tailed chestnut. He had been hunting for marmots and returned in the evening, after sunset, leading the horse which was laden with marmots swinging from the saddle.

His brothers told him about the theft of the geldings.

'I'll go after them!' said Belgutei, but Qasar said: 'Not you, you're not up to it. I'll go!'

---

* Without a tinder pouch, Temujin would not be tempted to stop for the night and make a fire. He was given only two arrows so that he could protect himself but could not engage in combat; and his horse was mediocre — possibly so that if he was caught there was nothing to connect him with Sorqan-shira.

† After Chinggis Khan's marriage to Borte, this became the 'First Palace'. His main camps all became 'Palaces' on the strength of his marriage alliances.

Then Temujin said: 'None of you shall go. This is my job.'

And he mounted the chestnut and set off, following the light bay geldings by means of their tracks in the grass.

For three days and nights he pursued them, and on the morning of the fourth day he met a strong, handsome youth, who was milking the mares in a large herd of horses. When he asked about the geldings, the young man said: 'Someone drove eight light bay geldings through here this morning, just before sunrise. Come, I'll show you where they went.'

He made Temujin leave the bald-tailed chestnut, giving him a black-backed grey instead. Then, without even going to his yurt, he hid his leather bag and bucket in the grass in the field, mounted a swift dun pony, and said:

'My friend, you have exhausted yourself on your journey. Your sufferings are mine, as are all men's. My father is Naqu the Rich and I am his only son. My name is Bo'orchu.* Come, I will go with you.'

For three days and nights they tracked the light bay geldings until, on the evening of the fourth day, they arrived at a large camp defended by a corral of carts. And there were the light bay geldings, grazing together at the edge of the camp.

'Stay here, my friend,' said Temujin, 'while I separate the geldings out and drive them over here.'

But Bo'orchu said: 'I came as your friend. Do you think I can stand here and watch you?'

So together they dashed in and drove out the light bay geldings.

Immediately the people rose in pursuit and came after them on horseback. One man on a white horse, carrying a pole with a lasso on the end, almost caught up with them, and Bo'orchu cried urgently: 'Give me the bow and arrow, my friend! Let me shoot at him.'

But Temujin called back: 'I'm not having you hurt for my sake. I shall exchange an arrow or two with him myself'; and so saying, he swung round in his saddle and fired. The man

* Bo'orchu later became one of Chinggis Khan's marshals, one of his 'Four Best Geldings' (see Appendix A).

on the white horse reined back, gesturing with his lasso, and his companions caught up with him; but even as they came level the sun set and dusk closed in. Soon their pursuers were out of sight, left behind in the darkness.

Temujin and Bo'orchu travelled all that night and for the next three nights until they reached Bo'orchu's yurt.

'My friend,' said Temujin, 'without you I couldn't have got my horses back. Let's divide them between us. It's only fair.'

But Bo'orchu said: 'You are my friend. When you arrived exhausted in my fields, it was as a friend I sought to help you. I chose to come with you, so how could I possibly seek a reward? My father is well-known and I am his only son. The riches he has are more than enough for me. If I expected a reward for helping you, what sort of help would that be? I don't want anything.'

They rode up to Naqu-bayyan's yurt, where they found the old man snivelling and weeping because he thought he had lost his son. As soon as he saw Bo'orchu, he alternately cried and scolded, until Bo'orchu said: 'Father, what is all this about? My good friend arrives exhausted. I go to help him. Now I am back.' And so saying he galloped off into the open fields to retrieve the leather bag and bucket which he had hidden there.

Then they killed a fat lamb for Temujin, strapped it to his horse, and tied a bag of kumiss to his saddle. As they made these provisions, Naqu-bayyan said: 'You two are young. Look after each other, and don't abandon each other!'

Temujin left, and after travelling for three days and three nights he arrived back at the yurt by the Senggur stream. By this time Ho'elun, Qasar and the rest of the family were beginning to worry, but when they saw him they rejoiced.

In 1178 Temujin and Belgutei set out on an important expedition. They went down the Kerulen river to look at Lady Borte, Dei-sechen's daughter, to whom Temujin had been promised when he was only nine years old. Dei-sechen of the Onggirat lived between two mountains, Chekcher and Chiqurqu, and when he saw the young men his heart rejoiced.

'I knew the Tayyichi'ut were jealous of you,' he said, 'and

I nearly despaired. But here you are at last!' With great ceremony Temujin was married to the Lady Borte, and afterwards Dei-sechen accompanied them as far as Uraq-chol on a bend of the Kerulen river. There he turned back, but his wife, Chotan, went on into the Gurelgu mountains to bring her daughter to Temujin's family.

After Temujin had sent Chotan home, he asked Belgutei to ride to Bo'orchu, saying: 'Let us be companions.' Bo'orchu was delighted, and without saying anything to his father rode back with Belgutei to Temujin's yurt,

> on a chestnut horse with a hunched back,
> his grey woollen cloak across the saddle.

And that is how Temujin and Bo'orchu became companions.

Soon after, they moved their camp from the Senggur stream to a place called Burgi-ergi, 'Muddy Banks', at the source of the Kerulen river. Borte's mother, Chotan, had given Temujin a dowry in the form of a black sable jacket, and the three brothers, Temujin, Qasar and Belgutei, took it and went off towards the Black forest. In earlier days their father, Yisugei, had befriended Ong Khan,* Lord of the Kereyit clan, and they had sworn eternal brotherhood.

'Anyone who swore eternal brotherhood with my father is like a father to me,' declared Temujin, and, knowing that Ong Khan was living down by the Tu'ula river, the brothers went to find him.

When they arrived, Temujin said: 'In days gone by you and my father swore eternal brotherhood, so you are like a father to me. I've just got married and this is my wife's dowry. I'd like you to have it.' So saying, he held out the black sable jacket.

Then the Ong Khan was greatly touched and said:

> 'In return for the black sable jacket
> I shall bring you the men who forsook you,
> in return for the black sable jacket
> I shall bring you the clans that are scattered.

---

* At this stage, To'oril Khan: he was given the title of Ong Khan after the battle with the Tatars (see Chapter Four).

From the depths of my bowels
to the bones of my breast
I give you my thanks.'

Back they went, and while they were camped on the banks of
the Burgi an old man of the Uriangqad clan called Jarchi'udai
came down from Burqan-qaldun carrying a pair of bellows
on his back and leading his son, Jelme. He came to Temujin
and said:

'When you were born on the banks of the Onon I gave you
swaddling clothes of sable. I also gave you my son Jelme, but
kept him in trust for you until he was older. Now put him up
on your saddle! Let him guard the door of your tent!' And so
saying, he ceremoniously handed Jelme over to Temujin.*

Early one morning, when the light of the dawning day showed
yellow, Qo'aqchin, an old woman who was working in
Mother Ho'elun's tent, suddenly roused herself.

'Mother, mother,' she cried, 'get up quickly. The whole
earth is shaking, and I can hear the pounding of swift horses'
hooves! The terrible Tayyichi'ut are coming! Mother, quickly,
rouse yourself!'

Lady Ho'elun was on her feet straight away. 'Quickly,' she
said, 'wake the children.'

Instantly alert, Temujin and the others leaped to their feet,
caught hold of their horses, and mounted. Temujin, Lady
Ho'elun, Qasar, Qachi'un, Temuge, Belgutei, Bo'orchu and
Jelme all took a horse apiece, and Lady Ho'elun gathered up
Temulun and set her in front of her on the saddle. There was
one horse over, but this was needed as a spare, so Lady Borte
was left without anything to ride.

While it was still early Temujin and his brothers struck
camp and rode off in the direction of Burqan. Meanwhile the
old woman, Qo'aqchin, hid Lady Borte in a black-covered
waggon harnessed to an ox with spots on his back.

They moved off upstream in the dim light of daybreak,
following the Tenggelik river, and as they went a group of

* Jelme later became one of Chinggis Khan's generals, his 'Four
Hounds' (see Appendix A).

soldiers trotted by and turned back to ask them who they were.

The old woman who was leading the ox said: 'I'm Temujin's servant. I came to shear sheep at the great yurt and now I'm going home to my own family.'

'Is Temujin there?' they asked. 'How far away is his yurt?'

'Not far,' said Qo'aqchin, 'but as for whether Temujin is there or not, I don't know. I left before daybreak by the back door.'

At this the soldiers trotted off. Then the old woman whipped up the ox with the spotted back and they set off again at a cracking pace. But alas! the axle of the cart broke.

'Look,' said she, 'the axle is broken. We'd better go into the forest on foot and run!'

But even as she said it the soldiers came back at a trot with Belgutei's mother mounted behind on one of their horses, her legs dangling.

'Come on,' they said, 'show us what you have in your cart!'

'Sheep's wool,' answered Qo'aqchin.

But the officers told their men to dismount and take a proper look, and when they lifted the door of the cart out they found what appeared to be a lady of rank sitting inside. They pulled her out, mounted both her and Qo'aqchin behind them on their horses, and took them away. Following Temujin's tracks in the grass, they went up towards Burqan-qaldun.

Three of the soldiers were of the Merkit family. They must have circled Burqan-qaldun three times but they couldn't find Temujin. They tried to penetrate the area but it was a mass of sinking mud and dense forest, and they were like glutted bears — unable to find their way in. They were right behind him, but they couldn't find him.

The names of the Merkit tribesmen were Toqto'a, Dayyir and Qa'atai, and they all came from different branches of the family. They wanted revenge because, all those years ago, Lady Ho'elun had been snatched from Chiledu and stolen away.

Now, frustrated, they said to each other: 'They took Ho'elun. We have taken their women. We have had our revenge.' And they came down Burqan-qaldun and went home with their prizes.

Meanwhile Temujin was wondering if the three Merkit had gone, or if they were still lying in wait. He sent Belgutei, Bo'orchu and Jelme to find out. The three men followed the Merkit for three days until they were sure they were rid of them.

Then Temujin came down from Burqan-qaldun and beat his breast. 'Mother Qo'aqchin', he cried,

> 'hears like a weasel,
> sees like a stoat.
> On the dotted tracks
> she saved my skin.

> I followed the deer trails,
> built yurts of willow,
> climbed on the Burqan,
> on Burqan-qaldun;
> just like an insect,
> a louse, I was hunted:
> alone I was spared.

> I followed the elk trails
> on one horse only,
> built yurts of twigs
> and climbed on the Qaldun,
> on Qaldun-burqan,
> and like a swallow's
> my life was granted.

I was afraid,' he said. 'I shall sacrifice to Burqan-qaldun every morning, and every day I shall pray to the mountain. And this shall be done even by the descendants of my descendants.'

Then, facing the sun, he draped his sash round his neck and hung his hat by its cord from his arm. And beating his chest with his hand and kneeling nine times to the sun, he gave up his offerings and prayers.

CHAPTER THREE

The rescue of Lady Borte.
A sworn brotherhood. Temujin
is chosen by his people
to become tribal khan.

WHEN THEY HAD FINISHED THEIR DISCUSSION
the three of them — Temujin, Qasar and Belgutei — went off
to visit To'oril, the Ong Khan of the Kereyit, who was at that
time living in the Qara forest beside the Tu'ula river. Temujin
told him:

'When we were still unfledged, three of the Merkit tribe
came and robbed me of my wife and my unborn son. Khan,
my father, can you save them for me? That's what I've come
to ask you.'

To'oril Khan replied: 'Didn't I tell you last time that you
could depend on me? Your father and I were sworn brothers,
and when you brought me the sable jacket you asked me to
be a father to you. When you put the coat round my shoulders
I gave you my answer:

> In return for this sable
> I will unite your scattered people,
> In return for this sable
> I will unite those who abandoned you.

And I said:

> From the depths of my breast
> I give you my thanks,
> from the depths of my bowels
> I give you my thanks.

Did you not hear my words? Now let me stand by them:

> In return for this sable
> I shall trample the Merkit;

'They gave Temujin the name of Chinggis Khan
and made him their lord' (*page 39*)

> Lady Borte shall be saved.
> In return for this sable
> I shall trample the Merkit;
> Lady Borte shall be rescued.

Now. Send a message to your younger brother, Jamuqa. He must be somewhere in the Qorqonaq forest. Tell him to take twenty thousand fighting men to form a left flank. Meanwhile, I'll set out from here with twenty thousand fighting men to form the right flank, and we'll meet at a time and place to be decided by him.'

So the three of them, Temujin, Qasar and Belgutei, returned to their yurt from To'oril Khan's camp, and as soon as they arrived Temujin sent the others to Jamuqa, saying: 'Tell my sworn brother that the Merkit came,

> That my bed is emptied by them,
> that my heart is broken by them.
> Are we not one family?
> How can we get revenge?
> Are we not blood brothers?
> How can we get revenge?'

This was the message he sent to Jamuqa, his sworn brother, and he added also the words of To'oril, the khan of Kereyit: ' "In former days your father came to my side when I needed him. Remember, Temujin, that I will be your friend in time of trouble. With twenty thousand men I shall protect your right flank in the battle; for twenty thousand more call on your brother, Jamuqa, and let him decide the time and place of meeting." '

When he heard these words, Jamuqa said: 'Temujin, my sworn brother,

> My heart aches
> to know your bed is empty;
> my liver aches
> to know your heart is broken.
> Let us in vengeance
> rescue our Lady Borte.
> Let us in vengeance

ravage the thieving Merkit,
break up the thieving Merkit
and bring her back,
bring back our Lady Borte.

Now,

The slap of saddle-flaps becomes
the beating of drums
to Toqto'a the Nervous
out on the Bu'ura steppe.
Dayyir-usun the Treacherous sees
the flexing bow and quiver
and he flees
to Talqun island
in the two great rivers.
Qa'atai the Disputatious
notes how the tumbleweed
takes refuge in the forest,
and follows its example.
Now he must be
already on the Qaraji steppe.

We must cut across the Kilqo river.
Let the abundant sedges
bind up our rafts;
let us go!

Toqto'a the Nervous—
we shall drop through your smoke-hole,
and crash through your door frame;
we shall pillage your women,
and murder your children,
and smash down your door frame,
destroying its sanctity,
robbing your people
until they are empty!'

And Jamuqa said again: 'Tell my sworn brother Temujin and
my elder brother To'oril that these are my words:

For my part I have pledged myself
to the spear-tipped banner,
have beaten the drum made of black bull's hide
till it rumbled like thunder.
I have put on my armour,
I have mounted my swift black horse,
I have grasped my steel-tipped spear,
And set my peach-bark arrow to the string.

Now let us ride;
let us strike at the Qa'at-Merkit!

Tell him this:

I have pledged myself to his banner,
and beaten the cow-hide drum
till it rumbled like thunder.
I have strapped on my armour of leather,
and mounted my swift grey horse.
With my hilted sword* in my hand,
I have set my notched arrow to the string.

Now to the death
let us fight with the Uduyit-Merkit.

And tell them this: that when To'oril, my elder brother, rides
forth he should make his way to Temujin by the south side of
the Burqan-qaldun, travelling up the Onon river to its source.
We shall meet there! I will go upstream with ten thousand
men to where ten thousand of my brother's people wait. We
shall meet at the source of the Onon river, and so farewell.'

Qasar and Belgutei returned to Temujin with Jamuqa's
message, and Temujin immediately relayed it to To'oril.
Accordingly, To'oril set out along the south side of the Burqan-
qaldun with twenty thousand men, and Temujin, anticipating
him, retreated upstream along the Tunggelik to give him
space. Gradually the three armies, led by To'oril, Temujin,
and To'oril's younger brother, Jaqa-gambu, converged, until

* Probably a sword made of two pieces, rather than forged out of
one.

at Ayil-qaraqana on the Kimurqa river, they pitched their camp together.

Then, with their armies, the three lords set out for the source of the Onon, where they found Jamuqa waiting for them. He had arrived at the appointed place three days earlier, and, after they had greeted one another, he was quick to confront them:

> 'If a meeting has been agreed
> neither snow nor rain
> should impede you
> or make you late.

Did we not agree a place and time? When the Mongols say "yes" are they not bound by an oath?

> Those who come late
> we cast out from the ranks!'

To'oril answered him, saying: 'You are right, younger brother, we are three days late at the appointed place and it is your duty to punish and rebuke us.' And they discussed their various grievances at the meeting.

From Botoqan-bo'orjin, they moved off to the Kilqo river, and, when they arrived, lashed rafts together to take them across to the Bu'ura steppe. At Toqto'a-beki's yurt they stopped

> and smashed their way in
> through doorway and smoke-hole;
> his wife and his son
> they robbed and then murdered;
> his sacred doorway
> they broke and defiled;
> his loyal people
> they crippled and looted.

Even as Toqto'a-beki* slept, some fishermen, sable hunters and sentries who had been down by the river ran through the

* *beki*: a high-ranking officer, entitled to ride a white horse and wear white clothing.

night to warn him of the danger. They roused him just in time: with a few of his men, he fled downstream to join Dayyir-usun of the Uwas-Merkit in Barqujin territory.

Then there was panic among the Merkit people. Down the Selengge river they ran at dead of night, closely pursued by our soldiers who robbed and killed anyone they overtook. And among those who followed was Temujin, crying aloud: 'Borte, Borte!'

Then Lady Borte, who was fleeing for her life, heard Temujin's voice and recognised it. She leaped from the still-moving cart and came running to him. Even in the darkness she and her maid could recognise the trappings of Temujin's horse, and together they seized the reins. By the light of the moon he saw her, and, as he jumped from his horse, he took her in his arms.

Then Temujin sent word to To'oril Khan and his blood-brother Jamuqa, saying: 'I've found what I was looking for. Let us forgo the chase for tonight and pitch camp here.' And so, as the Merkit clan had scattered in panic, they decided to pitch camp and rest there. That is how Lady Borte was saved by Temujin from the Merkit people.

Previously the three Merkit chiefs, Toqto'a-beki, Dayyir-usun and Qa'atai-darmala of the Three Hundred Men, had consulted each other, saying:

'It all began when Yisugei-ba'atur kidnapped the Lady Ho'elun from Toqto'a's younger brother. In revenge we circled Burqan-qaldun three times and captured Lady Borte from Temujin. We set Chilger-boko to guard her, and this he did at first. But after a while he abandoned her, saying:

> "The black crow,
> condemned to a diet of scraps,
> aspired to the flesh of goose and crane.
> So I, Chilger the Unfortunate,
> aspired to the Lady Borte
> and brought calamity
> on all the Merkit people!
> Ignoble Chilger,

bow your black head to receive the blow!
I have only one life to save;
I will creep into a black gorge,
but who will shield me?

The buzzard, that bad bird,
condemned to a diet of rats and mice,
aspired to the flesh of goose and crane.
So I, Chilger, doubly cursed,
became that lady's keeper,
bringing calamity
to all the Merkit people!
Oh Chilger, black, deformed,
bare your skull to the blow!
Your life's not worth sheep-shit,
yet I long to creep
into the darkest hole,
into the blackest gorge.
Your life is not worth sheep-shit.
Who will save me?"

And so saying, he turned and fled.'

Meanwhile Qa'atai-darmala had been captured. They put a wooden yoke on him and sent him off on foot towards Burqan-qaldun. Belgutei, who had heard that his mother was being held in that particular camp, immediately set off to rescue her. He found her yurt, but even as he went in through the right side his mother, dressed in ragged sheepskin, ran out through the left.

'I've been told my sons are khans now,' she said to a man outside, 'while I have been given to a commoner. How can I look them in the face?' And so saying she ran away and slunk into the thick forest. Belgutei searched for her frantically, firing horn-tipped arrows indiscriminately at the Merkit people.

'Bring back my mother,' he shouted.

By now the three hundred Merkit who had circled Burqan-qaldun, together with their children and their children's children, were as though they had never been. They were crushed and dispersed on the wind like ashes. Of the survivors, those who could be embraced — their women — were taken as concubines, and those who could serve indoors — their children — were taken as slaves.

Temujin gave respectful thanks to both To'oril Khan and Jamuqa:

'To'oril, my father; Jamuqa, my sworn brother: by Heaven and Earth and your friendship are my power and might increased:

> Appointed by Mighty Heaven,
> invited by Mother Earth,
> we have emptied the breasts
> of the Merkit, enemy of the people.
> Their livers we have torn in half,
> their beds we have emptied,
> their kinsmen we have destroyed,
> their survivors we have spared
> and then enslaved.'

'This is the story of the defeat of the Merkit people. It is done. Let us now withdraw,' they said to each other.

Meanwhile, as the Merkit were scattering in a panic, our soldiers found a small boy who had been left behind in the camp. He was only five years old, but there was fire in his eyes. His name was Kuchu, which means the Strong. He was dressed in a suit of suede otter-skins sewn together, with a hat of sable and boots made out of the skin of a doe's forelegs. The soldiers took him straight away to Mother Ho'elun and gave him to her as a battle-prize.

Then Temujin, To'oril Khan and Jamuqa came together and they

> razed the tents of the traders
> and plundered the tall-plumed women.

After that they withdrew from Talqun island, between the rivers Orqon and Selengge. Temujin and Jamuqa departed together towards the Qorqonaq forest, and To'oril Khan went to the north of Burqan-qaldun, crossing two passes, where he took time off to hunt wild beasts before returning to the Black forest on the Tu'ula river.

*

Meanwhile Temujin and Jamuqa pitched their camp together in the Qorgonaq forest. They remembered the oath they had sworn when Temujin was only eleven — to be blood brothers forever. On that occasion they had sealed their brotherhood by exchanging knucklebones — Jamuqa's came from a roebuck while Temujin's was bone filled with copper — and afterwards they had played each other on the icebound Onon river, calling each other 'Anda', which means 'Blood Brother'.

Afterwards, when the spring came and they went out to practise with their pinewood bows, Jamuqa gave Temujin a whistling arrowhead which he had made himself by gluing the horns of a two-year-old calf together and boring holes into it to make it sing. In return Temujin had given Jamuqa a horn-tipped arrow with a cypress butt. And once again they had renewed their oath.

Now they swore brotherhood for a third time. In olden days men used to say: 'Those who swear brotherhood share one life. They become joint protectors of that life and never abandon each other.' That was the way in which Jamuqa and Temujin loved each other, and they confessed their love and renewed the bond between them, saying: 'Let us love one another.'

During the war with the Merkit Temujin had looted a golden sash from Toqto'a, which he gave to Jamuqa. He also gave him Toqto'a's horse, a four-year-old fawn stallion with a black mane and tail. Jamuqa also had some plunder — a golden sash and a horse as white as a kid, with a horn on its forehead, which had belonged to Dayyir-usun — and these he gave to Temujin. There, by the Many-Leaved Tree on the south side of the Quldaqar cliff in the Qorqonaq forest, they pledged their love. A day of feasting followed, and then another, and that night they slept together under one quilt.

They stayed together for a year and a half. Then, one day, they decided to strike camp, and on the sixteenth day of the first month of summer — the Day of the Red Circle — they set off.

As the two men walked together in front of the waggons Jamuqa said:

> 'Shall we camp beside the mountain,
> ideal for our horses and our tents,
> or shall our home be by the river,
> with comfort for our shepherds and their stomachs?'

Temujin paused, not understanding the drift of Jamuqa's words. As he stood there in silence the convoy of waggons passed by him and he found himself beside the cart in which his mother, Ho'elun, was sitting.

'Mother,' he said, 'my sworn brother has just said these words to me:

> "Shall we camp beside the mountain,
> ideal for our horses and our tents,
> or shall our home be by the river
> with comfort for our shepherds and their stomachs?"

I didn't understand, so I did not answer him. I thought I'd ask you instead.'

Before Ho'elun could say a word, Lady Borte spoke:

'They say your sworn brother Jamuqa tires easily. Now it seems that he is tired of us. He has given us due warning: we should not camp with him, but move on. We should travel all night if necessary.'

Temujin took her advice. They rode all night without stopping, and in the middle of their journey they passed through Tayyichi'ut territory. The Tayyichi'ut people, alarmed at their coming, set off by mistake in the direction of Jamuqa's camp, but they left a small boy behind. His name was Kokochu, which means Seller of Herbal Medicines, and he was taken to Mother Ho'elun who brought him up as her own.

On they journeyed, and at daybreak they met the three Toqura'un brothers who had also been on the road. Gradually a crowd gathered: Qada'an-daldurqan of the Tarqut and his five brothers; Unggur, son of Monggetu-kiyan, and his followers; Qubilai and Qudus and their brothers from the Barulas. There were men from the Jalayir, from the Arulat, from the Besud, from the Urianqad, from the Qongqotan and from the Sukeken. There were men from the Ne'udei, the Olqunu'ud, the Qorolas, the Dorben and the Ikires. And among them were Qubilai and Sube'etei-ba'atur, who were to become Temujin's generals.

Then Qorchi came, saying: 'Jamuqa and I were born of one woman and shared one womb. I would never have left him but for an omen: I saw an off-white cow which came and circled round Jamuqa. First it butted his waggon, then it butted the man himself, breaking one of its horns on him.

'"Give me my horn," pleaded the cow, and repeated the plea again and again, bellowing and pawing the ground so that the air was thick with dust. And as the cow bellowed, so a yellow-white ox lifted up the great joist of the waggon, harnessed itself and set off along the great road. He was coming after you, Temujin. And he too bellowed repeatedly, saying: "Thus it is decreed by Heaven and Earth. Temujin shall be our master. Behold, I am bearing the nation to him."

'I myself saw the heavenly signs and heard the heavenly words. Temujin, when you are master of us all, how will you reward my prophecy?'

Then Temujin said: 'If what you have said is true and I am to be the master of this nation, then I will make you commander of ten thousand men.'

'How should that content me? Let me have more. Let me have the choice of your most beautiful and blameless girls, and let me make thirty of them my wives. And more: whenever I speak, turn your head and listen!'

Then Qunan came, leading the Geniges, and Daritai-otchigin after him. Tribe after tribe deserted Jamuqa to pitch their camp with Temujin at Ayil-qaraqana on the Kimurqa stream. And when Temujin felt that the defections were over, he moved his people into the Gurelgu mountains, to the Blue lake at Qara-jurugen.

In the year 1189, Altan, Quchar and Sacha-beki reached an agreement. They went to Temujin and said:

'We will make you khan,
and when you are khan

we shall gallop after all your enemies,
bring you girls and women of good complexion,

bring palace-tents and foreign girls with cheeks
like silk, bring geldings at the trot,
and give them to you.

We shall hunt for wary animals,
and drive towards you creatures of the steppe,
so that they brush against your very belly,
so that they press against your very thighs,
the creatures of the cliff.

In days of battle, should we disobey,
then from our wives and women cut us off,
then from our sacred families cut us off,
and batter our black heads upon the earth.

In days of peace, if we should disobey,
then from our men and servants exile us,
then from our wives and children exile us,
and banish us into the wilderness!'

Thus they swore, and they gave Temujin the name of Chinggis
Khan and made him their lord.

The first thing Chinggis Khan did was to allow Ogolei-
cherbi, Qachi'un-toqura'un, Jetei and Doqolqu-cherbi to
carry quivers. Then Onggur, Soyiketu-cherbi and Qada'an-
daldurqan came to him and said:

'You shall not lack your morning drink,
nor shall you lack your evening drink.'

And they became the chief cooks.

Next Degei said:

'I can make soup
from a two-year wether.
Pied sheep and brown ewes
shall I herd, and I shall fill
your folds and pens with sheep
that you shall sup
morning and evening.
Greedy I am, and useless too:
let me herd sheep for you
and eat their bowels!'

So Degei became a shepherd.

Then Degei's younger brother said:

> 'I shall take charge of the waggons,
> so that their lynchpins shall hold
> and their axles stay firm
> on the broad highway,

for I shall build the travelling carts.'

Then Dodai-cherbi added: 'I would like to be in charge of the women and servants.'

Then Chinggis Khan appointed his generals. He decreed that Qubilai, Chilgutei and Qarqai-tuqura'un, together with Qasar, should carry swords. Then to Belgutei and Qaraldai-toqura'un he said:

> 'Keep my geldings to hand
> and be my equerries!'

After that he decreed that the three Tayyichi'ut brothers, Qutu, Morichi and Mulqalqu, should herd the horses, while to four others — Arqai-qasar, Taqai, Sukegei and Cha'urqan — he ordered:

> 'Be my long-range arrows,
> Be my short-range arrows!'*

Then Sube'etei-ba'adur offered his services, saying:

> 'Like a rat
> I yearn to be part of the clan;
> like a black crow
> I want to scavenge with the clan.
> I shall become the felt over your head,
> the clan and I shall be the wind-break for your
> yurt.'

And after he had become khan, Chinggis said to Bo'orchu and Jelme:

> 'When I had no friends
> but my shadow,

* i.e. 'Take charge of my foreign and domestic affairs.'

> you became my shadows
> and brought me comfort.
> You shall live in my mind.'

And he added:

> 'When I had no fat
> but what was in my tail,
> you became my tail
> and gave me comfort.
> You shall live in my heart.

You stood by me then, and now you are greater than the rest. When Heaven and Earth decreed that my power should increase and gave me their protection, you were the men who chose me over Jamuqa. You proved my friends then and have now become my senior and most fortunate friends.' Then he added: 'I shall give each of you a different mission.'

Daqai and Sugegei were immediately sent as emissaries to To'oril, Khan of the Kereyit, saying: 'We have made your son Chinggis Khan.'

To'oril Khan answered and said: 'You have done well. The Mongols cannot live without a leader. Take my advice: never break the bond you have made, never upset the order you have established.' And so saying, he sent them home.

CHAPTER FOUR

The feast in the forest and the struggle for supremacy between the clans.

THEN CHINGGIS KHAN SENT ARQAI-QASAR and Cha'urqan to Jamuqa as emissaries, and Jamuqa gave them this message:

'Go to Altan and Quchar,' he said, 'and say this: "You have come between my sworn brother Temujin and myself. You have poked his flank and pierced his rib, and opened up a rift between me and my sworn brother. You should have made him khan when we were together. What do you want from him, now that he is khan?" Tell Altan and Quchar to keep their word now that they have pledged it. Tell them to cleave to my sworn brother and give him peace of mind.'

So saying, he sent them on their way.

Shortly afterwards, a young relation of Jamuqa's called Taichar, who was living on the south side of the Jalama mountain by the Olegei spring, set out with the express intention of stealing a herd of horses belonging to our ally Jochi-darmala. Taichar found the herd on the Sa'ari steppe and made off with it. As soon as Jochi realised this, he and his friends went in pursuit, but his friends soon lost heart and Jochi was left to go on alone through the night, until he saw the horses ahead of him. Then, lying flat along his horse's neck, he galloped into their midst and shot Taichar, breaking his back in two. When he had killed him, he rounded up his horses and drove them home.

The year was 1190. When Jamuqa heard that his brother was dead, he called all his men together. The Jadaran, his own tribe, combined with thirteen others to form an army of thirty thousand men, and together they rode out across the Ala'u'ut and Turqa'ut mountains against Chinggis Khan.

But Chinggis was forewarned. Mulke-totaq and Boroldai

of the Ikires came to his camp in the Gurelgu mountains and told him that Jamuqa was on the attack.

When Chinggis heard the news he too called together thirteen tribes to form an army of thirty thousand men, and these he led out against his old friend.

At Dalan-baljut they clashed for the first time, and Jamuqa had the better of the engagement. Chinggis and his men were forced to retreat into the Jerene gorge by the Onon river, and Jamuqa exulted, saying: 'We have driven him into hiding.' To mark his victory he boiled his captives alive in seventy cauldrons and, cutting off the head of Chaqu'au-u'a of Ne'udei, he tied it to his horse's tail and dragged it after him.

But though Jamuqa had won the first battle, it was not long before the Uru'ut and the Mangqut clans left him to join Chinggis Khan. Father Monglik of the Qongqotad also deserted him, and, with his seven sons, stole away to Chinggis's camp. Then Chinggis Khan rejoiced. At last the people were coming to him, and that night he, Lady Ho'elun and the others decided to hold a feast in the forest of Onon.

While they were feasting, a jug of kumiss was passed round. First Chinggis Khan drank, then Lady Ho'elun, then Qasar, Sacha-beki and the others. A second jug was poured and was handed first to Sacha-beki's 'little mother',* Ebegei. At that two of the ladies, Qorijin and Qu'urchin, protested:

'Why were we not served first? Why should Ebegei drink before us?'

And they set about the cook, Shik'ur, and beat him soundly.

'Why are you beating me?' cried the cook. 'Is it because Yisugei and Nekun-taishi, my former masters, are dead?' And he complained loudly.

While the feast was in progress, Belgutei had been left in charge of our people, while Buri-boko looked after the members of the Jirgin clan. Half way through, Belgutei caught a man stealing the tether from one of our horses, and, instead of agreeing to punish the thief, Buri-boko took his side and argued with Belgutei.

All his life Belgutei had been a champion wrestler, often

* i.e. His secondary wife.

removing his right sleeve to expose his naked arm. Now he took his sleeve off, and immediately Buri-boko slashed at his naked shoulder with his sword. The blood flowed, but Belgutei paid no attention to it. Then Chinggis, who had been watching the two men from the shadows, came forward. 'What does this mean?' he said. 'What has he done?'

Belgutei replied: 'The wound is nothing. Don't let it cause trouble between us and our kinsmen just when we're getting on so well. I'm not angry, and I shall soon recover. Let it be for the moment, brother.'

But Chinggis ignored Belgutei's advice and, pulling down branches from the trees and snatching the wooden paddles from their leather kumiss bags, he and his fellows set about the Jirgin and beat them soundly. They also took the two ladies prisoner, though they returned them later, saying: 'It would be better to settle our differences.'

While these negotiations were going on, Chinggis's spies brought him word that certain tribes, including the Tatars, were about to be attacked by Ongging-chingsang, commander of the Kitat people. He was advancing upstream, driving the Tatars and their leader Megujin before him, with all their livestock and provisions. When he heard this Chinggis said:

'The Tatars have been our enemies since ancient times, destroying our fathers and our fathers' fathers. We have reason enough to attack them.' And he sent a messenger to To'oril Khan, saying: 'They who destroyed our fathers and our fathers' fathers are now advancing on us. Let us mount a joint attack on them. Come quickly, my father!'

To'oril Khan lost no time. 'My son is right,' he said. 'Let us join him.'

Within three days he had assembled an army and set forth. He advanced rapidly, and, with Chinggis, sent joint word to Sacha-beki and Taichu of the Jirgin, saying: 'Now we have a good excuse for a joint attack on the Tatars — they who in former days destroyed our fathers and our fathers' fathers. Let us ride out together.'

Six days later, unable to wait any longer for a reply, Chinggis

Chinggis Khan amongst his followers:
'While they were feasting, a jug of kumiss
was passed around' (*page 43*)

Khan and To'oril Khan rode out at the head of their armies along the banks of the Ulja river.

Half way down the bank they found Megujin and his Tatars waiting behind a barricade, and swiftly overcame them. Megujin they executed there and then, and his soldiers were taken prisoner. Chinggis also took Megujin's silver cradle and his quilt which was hung with pearls.

The year was 1196. In triumph Chinggis Khan and To'oril Khan sent to Ongging-chingsang and told him that Megujin was dead. When Ongging-chingsang heard the news he rejoiced. On Chinggis he bestowed the title 'Ja'ut-quri', which means Commander, and to To'oril he gave the title 'Ong' or 'King'. This was how the title 'Ong Khan' originated.

Then Ongging-chingsang said: 'In defeating Megujin and killing him you have done my master, the Altan Khan, a great service. I shall report to him and he shall decide whether or not the title of "Jeu-tan" — Commissioner of Pacification — should be added to Chinggis's honours.'

Then Ongging-chingsang withdrew and rejoiced, leaving Chinggis and his father, the Ong Khan, to plunder the remaining Tatars. When they had finally divided the spoils, they went back to their own yurts and set up camp again.

While we were plundering the Tatar camp, however, our men found a small boy wandering round, abandoned. He wore a waistcoat of gold satin lined with sable and had gold rings in his ears and nose. The soldiers took him with them and Chinggis presented him as a victory prize to Mother Ho'elun.

'He must be a nobleman's son,' she said, 'he has that air about him.' So he became the younger brother to her five sons. She named him Shigiken-quduqu and brought him up as her own.

While Chinggis Khan was defeating the Tatars, he had pitched his base camp by the Hariltu lake, and, taking advantage of his absence, the Jurkin pounced. They killed ten of the men who had stayed behind in the camp and stole the clothing of another fifty.

When Chinggis Khan heard this he was furious, and said:

'Why should the Jurkin do such a thing? Remember our feast
in the forest when they beat the cook, Shiki'ur, and wounded
Belgutei in the shoulder? Even then we returned their women
to them and settled our differences peacefully. Then, when we
decided to attack the Tatars, arch-enemy of us all, they who
in former days destroyed our fathers and our fathers' fathers,
we waited six days for them and they did not come. Now,
instead of uniting with us against the enemy, they have become
the enemy.'

And so saying, Chinggis rode out against the Jurkin.

At that time the Jurkin had pitched their camp on Kodo'e
island in the Kerulen river. Chinggis Khan fell upon them,
plundering their people, while Sacha-beki and Taichu escaped
with only a handful of their men. Even then Chinggis pursued
them, and, catching up with them at the Teletu pass, he took
the leaders prisoner.

Then to Sacha-beki and Taichu he said: 'Have you forgotten
what we agreed in former days?'

The two replied: 'We did not keep our word. Make us keep
it now!' And they stretched out their necks for execution. But
Chinggis put up his sword when he heard them remembering
their oath, and, instead of shedding their blood shamefully,
he had them suffocated, as became their rank.*

Then, leaving their bodies where they lay, he went back
and took the Jurkin people in hand. Three sons of Telegetu-
bayyan of the Jalayir were with the clan at the time, and one
of them, Gu'un-u'a, brought two of *his* sons to Chinggis Khan
for an audience, saying:

> 'Let them be the slaves
> of your threshold;
> and should they leave your threshold,
> slice the sinews of their heels!
> Let them be the slaves
> of your tent-door,
> and should they leave your tent-door,
> cut out their livers and cast them out!'

* The Mongols believed that if their blood was shed they would be
unable to be reunited with their ancestors in Heaven.

And he gave his sons to Chinggis to be his servants.*

Then came Chila'un-qayyichi with his two sons, and he also begged an audience, saying:

> 'I give my sons to you.
> Let them be the guards
> of your golden door,
> and should they leave your golden door,
> cut their lives short and cast them out!
> I give you my sons.
> Let them lift for you
> your wide felt door,
> and should they ever leave you,
> kick in their hearts and cast them out!'

Then came Jebke, the third son, and he brought with him a small boy called Boro'ul. After an audience with Mother Ho'elun, he gave the child to her, while Chinggis gave Jebke to Qasar as a servant.

Mother Ho'elun now had four boys to look after, Guchu who had been found in the Merkit camp, Kokochu from the Besut camp, Shigiken-qutuqu who had survived the massacre of the Tatars, and Boro'ul from the Jurkin camp. She brought them up in her own yurt, saying to herself:

> 'These boys have become
> the seeing eyes of day,
> the listening ears of night . . .
>
> For whom am I doing all this?'

This is how the Jurkin got their name. The eldest of Qabul Khan's seven sons was Okin-barqaq, and when he came of age his father chose a tribe for him from among his own people. He picked

> those with gall in their livers,
> those who could shoot their arrows swift and far,
> those whose lungs were hearty,

* It was considered an honour to be a servant (i.e. slave) of the khan.

whose mouths were full of fury,
strong men who loved to wrestle,
fierce, peerless, arrogant and full of gall —
these men he gave to his son.

So the Jurkin clan was born and Chinggis Khan lost no time in bending this proud people to his will. Before long he had subdued and defeated them, making them his own.

One day Chinggis said: 'Let's make Buri-boko and Belgutei wrestle with each other.'

When Buri-boko had belonged to the Jurkin he had once challenged Belgutei and, holding him with one hand while he kicked at him with one foot, he had thrown Belgutei to the ground and kept him pinned down. Buri-boko had been the Jurkin's best wrestler, so Chinggis pitted the two of them against each other again. Buri-boko, who had never been beaten, let himself be thrown, but Belgutei could not wrestle him to the ground. Instead he grasped Buri-boko by the shoulders and jumped up onto his rump – for Buri-boko had buttocks like a horse. Then Belgutei caught sight of Chinggis Khan out of the corner of his eye, and, as he looked, the khan bit his lower lip. Belgutei understood. Crossing his hands in front of Buri-boko's neck and thrusting his knee into the small of his back, he jerked upwards, breaking the wrestler's spine in two.

Then Buri-boko, his back broken, said: 'I should not have let Belgutei beat me, but I was afraid of Chinggis Khan and my fear made me waver. I let Belgutei throw me and now I have lost my life.'

So saying, he died, and Belgutei dragged him away and cast him out. Buri-boko had been the son of Okin-barqaq's third brother, and he had been the Jurkin's best wrestler, but that was how he died, his back broken by Chinggis's man.

After this, in 1201, the Year of the Cock, several tribes united. The Qadagin, the Salji'ut and the Dorben, who had been allied with the Tatars, joined together, as did men from the Ikires, the Onggirat, the Qorolas and the sons of the Merkit, Oyirat and Tayyichi'ut. All these separate tribes gathered at the Alqui spring and decided to raise up Jamuqa as their chief.

They cut up a mare and a stallion and swore brotherhood with one another. Then, all together, they moved off down the Ergune river, and when they reached the wide plain where the Ergune joins the Kan they gave Jamuqa the title of 'Gur Khan', Lord of All. Then they began to plan their attack on Chinggis Khan.

Chinggis, meanwhile, was camped in the Gurelgu mountains, where he received a message from Qoridai of the Qorolas, telling him what was afoot. As soon as Chinggis heard the news, he alerted the Ong Khan, who swiftly sent his soldiers to Chinggis's aid.

After discussing their plan of campaign, both Chinggis and the Ong Khan set off down the Kerulen river to meet Jamuqa. Altan, Quchar and Daritai were sent ahead, as were Senggum, Jaqa-gambu and Bilge-beki—three from each army. Ahead of them went the scouts, establishing posts at Enegen-guiletu, Chiqurqu and Chekcher. The vanguard had got as far as Utkiya and were discussing whether or not to pitch camp there when a messenger galloped in from Chiqurqu to warn them that the enemy was approaching. Immediately the vanguard and their scouts rode out to meet them, to gather as much information about their movements as they could.

Before long we ran into Jamuqa's vanguard. As soon as we realised who they were, we shouted at them and they at us. Our men yelled: 'It's getting late. We'll fight tomorrow!' And we withdrew to spend the night with the main body of the army.

Next day the armies clashed at Koyiten. Lining up face to face, they drove each other first up the hill and then down, deploying their forces as best they could to gain ground. Then two members of Jamuqa's vanguard, Buyiruq Khan and Quduqa-beki, who were experts at using magic stones to bring rainfall, conjured up a huge storm. But the storm turned on them, crashing down so that they were unable to go on and tumbled back down the cliffs. Believing that the Heavens no longer loved them, Jamuqa's army scattered.

Buyiruq Khan immediately left the others and ran towards the Big mountain on Altai's southern flank. Qudu headed

for the Selengge, Quduqa struggled towards the forest and
A'uchu-ba'atur of the Tayyichi'ut made for the Onon river.
As for Jamuqa, he lost no time in plundering the very people
who had made him their chief, before he escaped downstream
along the Ergune.

As they scattered the Ong Khan pursued Jamuqa while
Chinggis went after A'uchu-ba'atur. As soon as he reached
the river A'uchu alerted his people, who immediately fled in
panic. But A'uchu himself called up his lieutenants and as
many extra men as they could muster, and lined up on the
far side of the river. They took up their square shields, and
deployed themselves in ranks, ready for battle.

Chinggis Khan was soon upon them and the battle with
the Tayyichi'ut began. Backwards and forwards they went,
thrusting at each other repeatedly until night fell. Then they
lay down on the very spot where they had been fighting and
slept cheek by jowl with the enemy until morning. Even those
who had fled earlier returned and pitched their camp on the
field of battle, side by side with the soldiers.

Chinggis Khan had been wounded that day: a vein in his
neck had been severed and he was worried that the blood
would not stop flowing. So, as the sun set and they camped
next to the enemy, Jelme began to suck the congealed blood
from his chief's wound until his own mouth was full of it. He
trusted no one but himself to look after Chinggis, but kept
guard over him, his mouth full of blood which he either swallowed or spat out. Then, past midnight, Chinggis regained
consciousness and said: 'The bleeding has stopped, but I am
terribly thirsty.'

At this, Jelme took off all his clothes, including his hat
and boots, and, wearing only his under-trousers, he ran into
the middle of the enemy camp. Jumping up onto the nearest
waggon, he searched for some kumiss but could not find
any: those who had fled had let the mares go without milking
them. Instead he took a large bowl of fermenting curds and
carried it back to his chief. Heaven must have protected him,
for no one saw him either coming or going. Then Jelme got
some water and, blending it with the curds, he made Chinggis
Khan drink. Three times he drank and then rested, until at

last he said: 'My mind and my eyes are clearing.' And as the khan sat up, dawn broke and light flooded in.

Chinggis looked around him. The first thing he saw was the congealed blood which Jelme had sucked and spat out: it lay like a mire all round him.

'What's all this?' asked the khan. 'Wouldn't it have been better to have spat a little further off?'

Jelme replied: 'I dared not go too far away. You were in an anxious state and I couldn't leave you. I swallowed what I could, the rest I spat out — all the same, I worried that so much went into my stomach.'

Then Chinggis Khan said: 'But you left me to go naked into the enemy camp. Suppose you had been captured? You would have been forced to tell them I was helpless.'

But Jelme answered: 'I had my story ready. I would have said this: "I wanted to come and join you but my fellows were suspicious. They threatened to kill me, and to stop me running away they took off my clothes. They were down to my under-trousers when I snatched at a chance to escape, so I came to you just as I am." They would have had no reason to doubt me: they'd have given me clothes and looked after me. With luck, I could have taken a horse from under their very noses and found my way back to you. That's what I thought. Anyway, my khan had a raging thirst and I wanted to satisfy it, so I went without blinking an eye.'

Then Chinggis Khan said: 'What can I say? You saved my life once before when the Merkit circled the Burqan mountain three times, looking for me. Now, by sucking my blood as it dried, you have saved my life again. What's more, you risked your own to quench my thirst, raiding the enemy camp without a thought for your own safety. And so for a third time you restored me to life. These three great services will live forever in my heart.' This he promised.

When day dawned, we found that some of the soldiers who were camping next to us had deserted during the night, while others had stayed where they were. Chinggis Khan immediately went in pursuit of the fugitives, and, as he was returning with them to the battlefield, he was stopped by a woman dressed in red who hailed him from the top of a ridge. 'Temujin!' she cried in a loud voice. 'Temujin!' And she wept as she stood there.

When Chinggis heard her, he sent a man up to the ridge to find out what was wrong.

She told him: 'I am the daughter of Sorqan-shira. My name is Qada'an. My husband was taken by your soldiers and as they were about to murder him I cried and wept for Temujin to save him for me.'

The messenger went back to Chinggis Khan, and, as soon as he had heard her words, Chinggis set off towards her at a trot. As he reached her he dismounted and, even though her husband was already dead by then — killed by our soldiers — they embraced each other.

Once his people had been rounded up Chinggis Khan decided to camp on that very spot with his main unit of soldiers. That evening he summoned Qada'un and made her sit beside him in his tent. On the following day, Sorqan-shira and Jebe, both of whom had been prisoners of war of the Tayyichi'ut, came to the camp, and to Sorqan-shira Chinggis said:

> 'Once you threw
> on to the ground
> the halter on my neck;
> once you removed
> the heavy wooden collar
> from my neck.

It was a great service you performed for me. Why have you tarried so long in joining me?'

Sorqan-shira answered: 'In my heart my trust in you was certain. But I could not afford to hurry. If I had come to you any earlier my Tayyichi'ut lords would have dispersed everything I left behind — wife, children, herds, possessions — like ashes to the winds. I was cautious and did not hurry, but now I am come to unite with my own khan.'

Chinggis Khan thought for a moment. 'You did the right thing,' he said.

Then he turned to Jebe:

'When we were fighting at Koyiten, circling round, deploying our troops, forcing each other to give ground, my yellow war-horse with the white mouth was shot from under me. And the arrow came from the top of that range. Who shot that arrow from the mountain top?'

Then Jebe answered: 'I shot the arrow from the mountain top. If it pleases the khan to put me to death here, then on a plot no bigger than the palm of a hand shall I be left to rot. But if the khan will grant me mercy, then shall I always ride ahead of him.

> I will attack:
> I will slash the deep waters
> and slice the shining stones.
> On your orders
> I shall take strongholds,
> breaking to pieces the blue stones.
> On your orders
> I shall invade,
> smashing to pieces the black stones.
> I shall attack.'

Chinggis Khan said: 'When a foe is faced with his enemies, with those he has killed, he usually keeps his mouth shut, too frightened to speak out. Not this man. Faced with his enemies, with those he has killed, he does not deny it, but admits it openly. That is the kind of man I want on my side. His name is Jirqo'adai, but because he shot my yellow war-horse with the white mouth in the neck, he shall henceforward be known as Jebe, which means "arrowhead". He shall be my arrow.'

So Jebe he became, and he walked at Chinggis Khan's side. His name was a reminder of the killing of Chinggis's horse, and of the khan's mercy. And that is how Jebe left the Tayyichi'ut to become Chinggis Khan's companion.*

---

* He later became one of Chinggis Khan's four great generals.

CHAPTER FIVE

Loyalties and treacheries. Chinggis Khan goes to war with the Tatar and Naiman tribes.

THEN CHINGGIS KHAN PLUNDERED THE TAYYICHI'UT and every tribe with Tayyichi'ut marrow in its bones. He killed the seed of the Tayyichi'ut people and dispersed them like ashes in the wind. Then he lined up those left behind and brought them with him to Quba-qaya, where he spent the winter.

One old man, Shirgu'etu of the Nichugut-Ba'arin, and his two sons saw the khan of the Tayyichi'ut running away from his tribe. 'He is our enemy,' they said, and they went after him and captured him. The khan's name was Tarqutai, which means the Fat One, and he was so fat he couldn't ride a horse, so they put him in their cart. On the way back they ran into Tarqutai's sons and younger brothers who had come out in a party to rescue him, and, as they drew level, the old man, Shirgu'etu, sat astride the khan, who was lying on his back in the cart. Then, still sitting on top of him and brandishing a knife, he cried:

'Here come your sons and younger brothers to rescue you. If I don't kill you, they'll execute me for having laid hands on their chief: if I do kill you, they'll execute me anyway. But if I must die, I shall take you with me as consolation!'

And, riding astride the khan, he made as if to cut his throat with his big knife. Then the khan cried out to his younger brothers and sons with a loud voice, saying:

'Shirgu'etu is going to kill me. What good will my corpse be to you then? Go back, before it's too late. Temujin won't kill me. It is said that when he was small he had

> fire in his eyes
> and light in his face!

Because of this I saved him when he had been abandoned in the camp.* I brought him home

> and I taught him.
> He was a quick learner;
> I taught him
> as though he were a young colt
> of two or three years old.
> I could have killed him then
> had I wished it ...
> Yet now they say
> that his knowledge shines forth,
> his mind breaks open ...

Temujin will not kill me. Go back quickly, my sons, my brothers, lest Shirgu'etu kill me first!'

Thus he shouted in a loud voice.

Then the rescue party said to one another: 'We came to save our father's life. If Shirgu'etu kills him, what good is his corpse to us? He hasn't killed him yet, so let's go back as quickly as we can.' And even as they debated the matter they turned back.

Meanwhile Alaq and Naya'a, Shirgu'etu's sons, who had been separated from him during the capture, rejoined their father and they all set off together. When they reached Quduqul-nu'u, Naya'a said:

'What will Chinggis Khan think when he sees that we have laid hands on our rightful lord? Won't he say: "How can they be trusted if they turn against their own chief? How can they be companions to us if they are not worthy companions to their own people? Those who plot against their lord should die!" Then he'll have us executed. Better we should release Tarqutai here and now and send him back. Then we'll go to Chinggis Khan and say: "We have come to serve you." And we'll tell him the whole story, saying: "We captured Tarqutai and were bringing him to you as our prisoner. But in the end we could not forsake our rightful khan. How could we kill our own lord? We have released him and let him go. But we

* There is no reference to this incident in any other source.

ourselves have put our trust in you and have come to offer you our power and might." Let us tell him this!'

The other two agreed with him. There at Quququl-nu'u they set Tarqutai free and sent him away. Then Shirgu'etu and his sons made their way to Chinggis Khan.

'Why have you come?' asked Chinggis Khan.

The old man replied: 'We captured Tarqutai and were bringing him to you as a prisoner. Then suddenly we thought: "He is our rightful khan; how can we forsake him?" So we let him go. But we ourselves desire to serve you, Chinggis Khan, and have come to offer you our power and might.'

Then Chinggis Khan answered and said: 'If you had laid hands on your own khan, Tarqutai, I would have executed you and all your brethren. No man should lay hands on his rightful lord. But you did not forsake him and your hearts were sound.'

This was Chinggis's answer, and afterwards he showed special favour to Naya'a.

After this Jaqa-gambu of the Kereyit tribe came to offer himself as a companion to Chinggis Khan. They were camped at Tersut, and at the same time the Merkit arrived to do battle with them. So Jaqa-gambu joined Chinggis Khan there and then in the struggle, forcing the Merkit army to retreat, and afterwards he persuaded the Tumen-Tubegen and the Olon-Dongqayit, scattered branches of the Kereyit tribe, to submit to his new lord.

In former days, when Yisugei Khan had been in power, he had lived in harmony with the Ong Khan of the Kereyit, and they had decided to swear brotherhood. This was how it came about. The Ong Khan had killed some of the younger brothers of his own father, and, as a result, one of his surviving bro-thers, Gur Khan,* rebelled against him. He had forced the Ong Khan to creep away and hide himself in the Black gorge. So, with only a hundred men, the Ong Khan had made his way to Yisugei Khan and had asked for his help. Together,

* NB. Neither of the Gur Khans in this story should be confused with Jamuqa, who was given the same title.

on horseback, they chased Gur Khan towards Qashin; then Yisugei rounded up the Ong Khan's kinsmen and returned them to him. As a result they swore brotherhood to one another.

After this the Ong Khan turned his attention to another of his younger brothers, Erke-qara, and sought to kill him; but Erke-qara escaped and went to Inancha Khan of the Naiman tribe for help. Inancha Khan sent out an army; but in the meantime the Ong Khan had gone to the Gur Khan of the Qara-kidat. Travelling by way of three cities — Tangqut, Uighur and Kitan – he found him and promptly fomented rebellion against him. He relied on five goats for milk, tethering them in a line, and on the blood of his camels for sustenance, but by the time he reached Lake Guse'ur in 1196, he and his men were very weak.

Then Chinggis Khan, remembering that the Ong Khan had formerly sworn brotherhood with his father Yisugei, sent ambassadors to him, and even went in person to meet him. Seeing him hungry and thin, Chinggis Khan raised levies for him and took him into his own camp. The Ong Khan stayed with him and together they wintered at Quba-qaya.

But the surviving brothers of the Ong Khan, and their lords, were dissatisfied, and said among themselves:

'This khan, our brother, has a bad character. His liver stinks inside him. He's got rid of his own flesh and blood, joined the Qara-kidat, and has made his people suffer. What shall we do with him? Shall we talk of former days, when he was only seven and the Merkit people captured him and took him away? They gave him a jacket of black spotted kidskin then, and made him grind grain in the Merkit mortar. Then his father came and attacked the Merkit people and rescued his son.

'When he was only thirteen, he and his mother were captured by the Ajai Khan of the Tatar tribe. This time he was made to look after the camels until Ajai's shepherd helped him to escape. After that he ran away into the Sarta'ul region, for fear of the Naiman people. He threw himself on the Gur Khan's mercy, only to rebel against him before a year had passed. Then he wandered in the lands of the Uiqut and the

Tangqut, getting weaker and weaker. He lived on the milk of five goats tethered in a line, and on the blood of his camels. And when all that remained to him was a blind yellow horse with a black mane and tail, he came to Temujin and called him son. So Temujin raised levies for him and supported him — and how does the Ong Khan repay him? By forgetting what he has done, and by going round giving vent to his stinking bile. What shall we do with him?'

But Altun-ashuq, who had been a party to their discussion, reported them to the Ong Khan, saying: 'Although I took part, I can't forsake you now, my khan.'

Then the Ong Khan seized his lords and all his younger brothers save one — Jaqa-gambu — who escaped and joined the Naiman tribe. The others were tied up and thrown into an old yurt where the Ong Khan came to them and said:

'What did we decide when we were travelling through the lands of the Uiqut and the Tangqut? Would you like to know what I think of you and your kind?' And he spat in their faces. Then he loosened their bonds and ordered everyone around to stand up and spit on them.

The winter was spent at Quba-qaya, but in the autumn of the Year of the Dog, 1202, Chinggis Khan prepared to do battle with four of the Tatar tribes at Dalan-nemurges.

Before the battle he gave orders to his soldiers, saying: 'If we triumph, we should not stop for booty, but press home our advantage. Once victory is secure, the booty will be ours anyway, won't it? Then we can divide it amongst ourselves. If we are forced to retreat, let us regroup in the original spot where we began our attack. Anyone who does not come back will be executed.'

These were his orders, which were agreed with his men beforehand. Then the battle began and the Tatars were driven back. After victory was secure, the enemy soldiers were forced to join their people by the Uluqui-shilugeljit river and there they were plundered and looted. The Chaqan-tatar, the Alchi-tatar, the Duta'ut-tatar and the Aluqui-tatar were completely wiped out, but although Chinggis Khan had made himself clear before the battle, three men had failed to obey orders and had stopped for booty. Displeased that his words had been ignored, Chinggis Khan sent Jebe and Qubilai to confiscate horses, goods, everything, from those who had taken them.

After he had crushed the Tatar tribes and plundered them remorselessly, Chinggis Khan called a major meeting of his own people to decide what should be done with the survivors. He and his men went into a huge yurt and held a council:

'From early days' (they said to each other) 'the Tatar tribes have destroyed our fathers and our fathers' fathers. We must be revenged! We will stand them against a lynchpin and kill anyone who is taller. We will completely destroy their fighting men. Then we will make the survivors our slaves, dividing them amongst us.'

As they emerged from the yurt after the meeting, Yeke-cheren of the Tatars asked Belgutei what verdict they had reached.

Belgutei said: 'We are going to measure you all against the lynchpin and kill anyone who is taller.'

When Yeke-cheren told his people what Belgutei had said, they immediately built a barricade against our soldiers. We surrounded it and attacked the Tatars, sustaining heavy losses. It proved extremely difficult to overcome them and finish them off against the lynchpin because the Tatars had said to each other: 'Let every man hide a knife in his sleeve. Then, if we must die, we will take them with us!' For this reason we suffered heavy losses, but finally we measured them all against the lynchpin and finished them off.

Then Chinggis Khan issued a decree:

'We have lost many men, and all because Belgutei told the Tatars what we had decided in council. From now on Belgutei shall be excluded from major councils — he will remain outside and take charge of other matters. It will be up to him to judge those who have stolen or lied. Only when our conference is over, and the ceremonial kumiss drunk, shall Belgutei and Da'aritai be admitted.'

This he decreed.

Then Chinggis Khan took a bride, Lady Yisugen, daughter of the Tatar Yeke-cheren. Knowing that Chinggis loved her, Lady Yisugen said to him: 'If I find favour with the khan, then he will surely look after me, whether he looks upon me as a human being or as a beast of burden. But my elder sister, Yisui, is above me — perhaps she would be more suitable to be the wife of a khan. Recently a son-in-law was added to our family, but in this confusion I don't know where anyone is.'

Chinggis Khan listened to her words, then answered: 'If your sister is above you, let us search for her. If we can find her, will you yield your place to her?'

And Lady Yisugen said: 'If the khan will show me his favour, and I may see my sister first, then I will give up my place.'

Chinggis Khan agreed to her terms and sent out a decree that Yisui should be found as soon as possible. Our soldiers spread out and soon caught her slipping away from her tribe with the son-in-law the family had given to her. He escaped; but Yisui was captured and brought back.

When Yisugen saw her elder sister she kept her promise, and, rising from her seat, gave it to Yisui. Then she herself went to sit lower down, while Chinggis Khan, seeing that Yisui matched her sister's description, took her to his heart. He married her, and made her sit with his other wives as their equal.

One day, after he had finished plundering the Tatar people, Chinggis Khan was sitting outside, drinking with his friends. And as he sat drinking between Yisui and Yisugen he heard Yisui sigh deeply. This caused Chinggis Khan to think, and, having thought, he summoned Bo'orchu, Muqali and the other lords to him.

'Line up all the people, tribe by tribe,' he decreed, 'and separate our own people from the others.'

When they had lined them up, tribe by tribe, one good-looking young man was left, standing by himself. They asked him who he was and he replied:

'I am the man who was given to Yisui as a son-in-law. I was afraid of the enemy so I ran away, but when things had calmed down I thought it would be safe to come back. I thought I wouldn't be recognised among all these people, so back I came.'

'Then Chinggis Khan plundered
the Tayyichi'ut, and every tribe with
Tayyichi'ut marrow in its bones' (*page 54*)

'"We ourselves desire to serve you,
Chinggis Khan, and have come to offer you
our power and might"' (*page 56*)

When they reported the young man's words to Chinggis, he issued a decree, saying:

'He thinks like an enemy, and he wanders around like a bandit. What is he doing here? We took all the men like him and measured them against the lynchpin — why should he be different? Take him away!'

So he was taken away and summarily executed.

In that same Year of the Dog when Chinggis Khan was at war with the Tatar people, the Ong Khan went to war with the Merkit. He drove Toqto'a-beki down towards the Barqujin plain and killed his eldest son, Togus-beki. Then he took the two daughters as his wives and plundered the other sons: indeed, he plundered all Toqto'a-beki's people. But he never shared any of the booty with Chinggis Khan.

After that Chinggis and the Ong Khan set out to do battle with Buyiruq Khan of the Guchugud Naiman tribe. They found him at Soqoq-usin by Uluq-taq, but Buyiruq Khan, instead of facing them in battle, fled over the Altai mountain. Chinggis's army pursued him, and, forcing him to cross the mountain, they chased him downstream along the Urunggu river by the Qum sand-hills. During the chase, Yedi-tubluq, a man of high rank who was serving as one of Buyiruq's scouts, was pursued by our men and taken prisoner. Meanwhile Chinggis and the Ong Khan caught up with Buyiruq himself at the Kishil-bashi lake and there they finished him off.

Chinggis and the Ong Khan turned back after the chase, but in the meantime the warrior Kokse'u-sabraq had reorganised the Naiman army and deployed it ready for battle at the Bayidaraq confluence. Chinggis Khan and the Ong Khan were happy to fight and deployed their own troops accordingly, but by the time they arrived it was getting late.

'Let us fight tomorrow,' they said, and they spent the night lined up as they were, ready to do battle in the morning. The Ong Khan lit fires on that very spot, but during the night he moved away upstream along the Qara-se'ul. As he went Jamuqa joined him, and presently Jamuqa spoke in the Ong Khan's ear, saying:

'Earlier my sworn brother Temujin sent messengers to the

Naiman clan, and now he declines to join us. Khan, oh Khan, I am the lark that stays close to you while my sworn brother is a lark afar off. Perhaps he has joined the Naiman instead, and that is why he does not come with us.'

Then Gurin-ba'atur of the Ubchiq tribe overheard Jamuqa's words and said:

'Why does he flatter the Ong Khan like this, slandering and insulting his honest brother?'

Meanwhile Chinggis Khan spent the night where he was, in preparation for the battle next day. When dawn broke, he saw that the place which the Ong Khan and his army had occupied was deserted.

'They have made burnt offerings of us,' he said. And he moved his army out and crossed the point where the Eder and Altai rivers meet. On he went until he reached the Sa'ari steppe, where he pitched his camp. At that moment, Chinggis and his younger brother Qasar, having taken stock of the military situation, realised that the Naiman were a people not worth fighting.

But Kokse'u-sabraq was following the Ong Khan, and he succeeded in capturing the Ong Khan's son's wife and daughter, taking them prisoner and plundering the family. Then he ambushed half the Ong Khan's people at the mouth of the Telegetu pass, and dispossessed them of their herds and provisions before he withdrew. During this battle, Qutu and Chila'un, the sons of Toqto'a of the Merkit, took their own people and departed, going downstream along the Selengge river to join their father.

Then, after his treatment at the hands of Kokse'u-sabraq, the Ong Khan sent a messenger to Chinggis Khan, saying:

'My clan, my wife and my sons have been plundered by the Naiman tribe. I beg you, my son, to send me your four best geldings'* (and by this he meant Chinggis's four best warriors) 'to save my people!' That was the message that the Ong Khan sent.

Then Chinggis Khan rallied his soldiers and called together his four best geldings, Bo'orchu, Muqali, Boro'ul and Chi-

* See Appendix A.

la'un-ba'atur. By the time they arrived at Hula'an-qut, the Ong Khan's son was on the point of being captured — his horse had been shot through the flank with an arrow. Chinggis's warriors saved him in the nick of time, and restored everything to him — his clan, his wife and his children.

Then the Ong Khan said: 'In former times his father restored my scattered people to me. Now, with his four best geldings, the son does the same, and gives me my scattered people again. Let Heaven and Earth bear witness to the way in which I repay my debt.'

And again he said: 'Once, Yisugei-ba'atur, my sworn brother, restored to me my scattered people. Now Temujin, his son, has gathered them together and given them back to me. Father and son have gathered my scattered people and given them to me. Why should they have thus gathered and given and suffered on my behalf? Now

> I grow old.
> I shall go up to the heights.
> And when, grown old,
> I climb those rocky slopes
> who will be
> the father to my people?

My younger brothers have no strength of character, and Senggum, my only son, is worse than none at all. I shall ask Temujin to be Senggum's elder brother; then I shall have two sons to my name, and I shall be at ease.'

So the Ong Khan met Chinggis Khan in the Black forest on the Tu'ula river, and they declared themselves to be father and son.

This was the reason, as you have already heard. Long before, Yisugei, Temujin's father, had sworn brotherhood with the Ong Khan and the Ong Khan had become a father to Temujin. So now they declared themselves father and son. They also spoke of other things:

'When we are riding out against our enemies,' they said, 'let us have one goal in mind. When we are hunting the wild beasts, let us have a single aim in view.'

And as they talked, they realised that the others would be jealous of them:

> 'Should we be stung
> by a snake's tooth,
> let it not penetrate:
> let us understand each other,
> by teeth, by mouth
> let us trust each other.
> Should we be slandered
> by a snake's back tooth,
> let us reject the slander:
> let us understand each other,
> by mouth, by tongue
> let us trust each other.'

And they kept their word, living together in friendship.

'On top of friendship, let there be double friendship,' declared Chinggis Khan, and he suggested that it would be a good idea to ask for Senggum's younger sister as a bride for his son Jochi. In exchange, he would offer our Qojin-beki to Senggum as a wife for his son Tusaqa.

Then Senggum, who had a high opinion of himself, said: 'If a girl from our clan joins Chinggis's people, she will find herself standing by the door-fire, looking into the tent, facing north; whereas if one of his women comes to us, she will take precedence, sitting at the back of the tent and looking towards the door-fire, facing south.'

And, in his arrogance, Senggum rejected the idea of such an alliance. 'We shall not give Cha'ur-beki to you,' he said.

Chinggis Khan was much displeased by these words, and was inwardly disappointed in the Ong Khan and the Ong Khan's son.

Jamuqa realised that Chinggis was disappointed. In the spring of the Year of the Pig, 1203, he joined Altan, Quchar, Qardakidai, Ebugejin, Noyakin, Soge'etei, To'oril and Qachi'unbeki, and together they went to see the young Senggum. They found him at Berke-elet on the northern side of the Jeje'er heights, and Jamuqa lied to him, saying:

'My sworn brother Temujin is sending messages to the Tayang Khan of the Naiman clan. His mouth may say the words "father" and "son" but his heart says no such thing. How can you be so trusting? Unless you mount a surprise attack on him, anything could happen. If you ride out against my sworn brother, I will join your attacking flank.'

Then Altan and Quchar said:

> 'We are sons of Mother Ho'elun,
> for you we will kill the elder brother,
> for you we will lay waste the younger brothers!'

And Ebugejin, Noyakin and Qardakidai said:

> 'For you we will seize his hands
> and trip his feet!'

To'oril said: 'Let us find some way of separating Temujin from his people. Without his people he can do nothing.' And Qachi'un-beki said:

> 'Whatever you decide, my son,
> I will go with you
> to the bottom, to the depths.'

When he heard these words Nilqa-senggum (which means 'younger son') sent a messenger to his father. The Ong Khan, on hearing what had been said, was angry.

'How can you entertain such thoughts about my son Temujin?' he said. 'Until now he has given us nothing but support. If you ponder wickedness against him, Heaven will not look on us with favour. Jamuqa has a slanderous tongue. Is what he says right? Is it decent?'

He was extremely displeased and sent the messenger back.

Then Senggum sent word again to the Ong Khan: 'I send men to you with eloquent tongues. Why don't you believe me?'

Twice or three times he sent the same message, until eventually he grew weary and went to his father himself.

'Father, Temujin gives us no consideration even now while

you are still living. Truly, my father, can you expect him to allow us to govern our people when your milk chokes you and you gag on your meat? These are the people your father toiled to bring together. Will he ever let us govern them after you are gone?'

To these words the Ong Khan could only reply: 'My child, how can I forsake my own son? Till now he has never failed in his support. How can we ponder wickedness against him? Heaven will not love us for it!'

At this Nilqa-senggum was angry, and, throwing aside the felt door of the yurt, he strode out. But the Ong Khan's heart went out to his son Senggum, and he bade him return. 'Heaven will not love us,' he repeated. 'How can you ask me to forsake Temujin? Nevertheless, you must do as you think best and you know this.'

It was the year 1203. Senggum said:

'They have asked us for Cha'ur-beki's hand in marriage, and if we grant it they will all come to the Sheep Neck feast.* So let us fix a day, invite them to the betrothal and capture them.' Everyone agreed with Senggum's plan, and they sent word to Chinggis Khan: 'We will give you Cha'ur-beki. Come and attend the Sheep Neck feast!'

So Chinggis came, with ten of his men. But on the way they spent the night with Father Monglik in his yurt, and Father Monglik said:

'When we asked for Cha'ur-beki before, these very people refused. Now, for no apparent reason, they change their minds and summon us to a betrothal feast. These people have a high opinion of themselves, so why have they suddenly offered you the girl? Are their motives straight and true? My son, you must plan your movements carefully. Send an excuse; tell them spring is coming, the horses are getting thin and need moving to better pasture.'

So Chinggis did not go. He sent Buqatai and Kiratai to the feast, and told them to eat, while he went back to his people.

* Betrothal feasts were so called because it was hoped that the marriage would prove as durable and tough as a sheep's neck.

As soon as they saw Buqatai and Kiratai, Senggum and his friends knew that they had been discovered. 'Early tomorrow we will surround them all and take them prisoner,' they said.

So they made their plan and agreed upon it. But when Altan's younger brother, Yeke-cheren, returned to his yurt he said to his wife:

'We have decided to take Temujin by surprise early tomorrow. If someone were to go to him with a message, I wonder what would become of him?'

His wife said: 'You shouldn't speak so loosely — people may believe what you say!'

And, indeed, while they were talking Yeke-cheren's herdsman, Badai, who had come to deliver the milk, overheard them. He went straight to his friend, Kishiliq, and told him what had been said. Kishiliq said: 'I'm going to find out for myself.'

So he went to the yurt where he found Yeke-cheren's son, Narin-ke'en, sitting outside, sharpening his arrows and saying to himself: 'Remember what we said just now? Our tongues should be cut out, because now we can't stop anyone talking about it.'

Then he turned to Kishiliq the herdsman and said: 'Capture the white horse of the Merkits and the bay with the white muzzle, bring them here, and tether them ready. Tomorrow morning, early, we ride out to attack.'

Then Kishiliq went back to Badai and said: 'I've checked what you said and it's true! It's up to the two of us to go and warn Temujin.'

So they agreed, and taking the white Merkit horse and the bay with the white muzzle they tethered them near at hand. Late that night they killed one of the lambs in their travelling tent and cooked it with wood broken from their bed. Then, mounting the two horses, they rode off into the night. They arrived at Chinggis's camp while it was still dark and crept up to his yurt from behind.* Then Badai and Kishiliq told Chinggis everything they had heard from Yeke-cheren and his

---

* By talking to Chinggis Khan through the thin felt wall at the back of the yurt, Badai and Kishiliq could ensure a measure of privacy.

son while they were sharpening their arrows. 'If the khan favours us,' they said, 'he will believe our story. They plan to attack you tomorrow and take you prisoner.'

CHAPTER SIX
The Ong Khan and Jamuqa, his former allies, declare war on Chinggis Khan. They are reprimanded for their disloyalty.

WHEN HE HEARD WHAT BADAI AND KISHILIQ had to say, Chinggis Khan believed them. That same night he sent a message to those of his people whom he trusted. Leaving their belongings behind and travelling light, they stole away that very night, going along the northern edge of the Evil heights. Chinggis asked Jelme-go'a, whom he trusted, to stay behind and guard the heights; then he posted scouts and moved on. They travelled all night, arriving next day at Qalaqaljit sands where they stopped at noon to rest and refresh themselves. There they stayed until the sun began to sink.

While they were resting, Alchidai ordered his herdsmen, Chigidei and Yadir, to take his geldings to some new pasture farther off, and as they herded the geldings they saw the dust of enemy horses coming up the southern side of the Evil heights.

'The enemy is coming!' they shouted, and, driving the geldings before them, they rode back to the camp to warn Chinggis Khan. Then the khan saw for himself the dust raised by the enemy as they came up through the Red bushes on the south side of the Evil heights.

'That is the Ong Khan,' he said, 'and he's coming after us.'

Immediately he ordered the horses to be loaded up and they all rode off. If the herdsmen had not spotted the enemy when they did, Chinggis and his men could easily have been taken by surprise.

Meanwhile Jamuqa was riding beside the Ong Khan, who presently asked him: 'Who are my son Temujin's most likely warriors?' And Jamuqa replied: 'The Uru'ut and the Mangqut clans: they are real fighters —

> Every time they turn around
> they are ranged for battle,
> every time they turn about
> they are poised to fight.

These people are born to swords and spears, to white banners and coloured banners. They are not of our caste.'

To these words the Ong Khan said:

'In that case we will send Qadag to meet them. He and the other Jirgin shall form the vanguard, while Achiq-shirun, who is stern and full of anger, shall follow him with the Tumen-tubegen warriors. Behind them shall come the Olon-dongqayit, followed by Qori-shilemun-taishi, with my body-guard of a thousand men. And after them shall come the main core of our army. And now, Jamuqa,' he added, 'as you are our younger brother, it is up to you to give orders to our men.'

At this point Jamuqa found himself standing apart, so he went to his friends and said: 'The Ong Khan has told me to take command. I know I can never defeat my sworn brother Temujin, yet he puts me in command. He is worse than I am, a fair-weather friend. I shall send a message to my sworn brother Chinggis Khan telling him to hold firm.'

So Jamuqa sent a message secretly to Chinggis Khan, saying: 'The Ong Khan has asked me: "Who are the warriors who will fight for my son Temujin?" I told him I thought you would put the Uru'ut and the Mangqut in the vanguard. As a result he has decreed that the Jurkin should form our vanguard, with Achiq-shirun of the Tumen-tubegen to back them up. They will be followed by the Olon-dongqayit and the Ong Khan's own bodyguard of a thousand soldiers. The main core of the army will come in the rear. Then the Ong Khan called me his younger brother and told me to take command. He said he relied on me; and I realised at that moment that he was only a fair-weather friend. How can I give orders to his troops? I will not fight against my sworn brother. But the Ong Khan is even less capable than I am, and therefore, my sworn brother, you must stand firm.'

After he had heard Jamuqa's message, Chinggis Khan spoke to his uncle Jurchedei of the Uru'ut tribe.

'What do you say, Uncle? Shall I put you in the vanguard?'

Before Jurchedei could say a word, Quyildar-sechen of the Mangqut spoke up:

'I want to defend my sworn brother. I'll trust him to look after my orphaned children if need be.'

Then Jurchedei said: 'We both want to fight in front of Chinggis Khan,' and so saying the two commanders ordered their troops to line up before their chief. They had hardly deployed the vanguard before the first wave of enemy troops attacked. Chinggis's soldiers counter-attacked immediately, crushing the Jirgin warriors. But even as they defeated them, the Tumen-tubegen appeared, and in the skirmish their leader, Achiq-shirun, pierced Quyildar's battle-gear with a lance and toppled him off his horse. Then the Mangqut withdrew and stood over Quyildar while Jurchedei's men crushed the Tumen-tubegen comprehensively. The Olon-dongqayit counter-attacked, but Jurchedei was ready for them, and beat them soundly. Even as he pressed home his advantage, Qori-shilemun-taishi attacked at the head of the Ong Khan's body-guard, but Jurchedei forced them back and crushed them in their turn.

Now Senggum, without consulting the Ong Khan, plunged into the fray, only to be shot in the cheek by an arrow. He fell on that spot and the Kereyit soldiers retreated to surround and protect him where he lay. Now there was nothing to stop our soldiers: we went forward and crushed them all, and, as the sun set, touching the tops of the low hills, our soldiers turned back. Carrying the wounded Quyildar, we left the Ong Khan on the field of battle, and found a place to spend the night further off.

We passed the night on the alert: but when we took the roll-call next morning Ogodei, Boro'ul and Bo'orchu were found to be missing.

Chinggis Khan said: 'Bo'orchu and Boro'ul are our trusted brethren. They must have stayed behind with Ogodei. Living or dying, how could those three desert one another?'

During the night our soldiers rounded up the geldings, and

Chinggis Khan said: 'If they try to attack us from the rear we must be ready to fight!' So the men stood ready, obeying his orders.

When dawn broke, we looked and saw one man coming up behind us, and as he got nearer we saw that it was Bo'or-chu! Then Chinggis Khan beat his breast and said: 'Let the Almighty Spirits of Eternal Heaven guide our fate.'

And Bo'orchu told his story:

'While we were attacking, my horse fell, shot by an arrow. So I ran forward on foot, and as I ran the Kereyit turned back to protect their leader, Senggum. There was a lull in the fighting, and I found a pack-horse — its load had slipped and the horse was just standing there. I cut the pack away, mounted the pack-saddle and rode away. By then our men had left the battle-field. I followed their tracks and here I am.'

Shortly afterwards, another man appeared on horseback. As he came closer it looked as though he had a second pair of legs dangling under him, and when he finally reached them they saw that Boro'ul was riding behind Ogodei on one horse. As Boro'ul reined in, our men saw blood trickling from the corner of his mouth. Ogodei had been hit in the neck by an arrow, and Boro'ul had been sucking the blood from the wound and letting it trickle away from the corners of his mouth. When Chinggis Khan saw them both, his heart bled for them and tears fell from his eyes. He quickly ordered a fire to be made so that Ogodei's wound could be cauterised. Then he asked for something to drink and gave it to Ogodei himself.

'If the enemy comes, we will fight,' he said again; and Boro'ul answered: 'You can see the dust trail of the enemy over there, moving towards Hulu'an-buruqut by the southern side of the Evil heights. They have left a long trail behind them.'

To these words Chinggis replied: 'If they come, we will fight. If we are forced to retreat, then we will regroup our forces and attack once more.'

With these words he gave the order to move out, and they went on their way, travelling upstream along the Ulqui-shilugeljit river until they came to Dalan-nemurges.

*

Shortly afterwards, Qada'an-daldurqan left his wife and children and came to Chinggis Khan's camp. He told Chinggis what had been happening:

'The Ong Khan's son, Senggum, fell, shot in the cheek with a round-tipped arrow, and the Ong Khan's men turned back to protect him. Then the Ong Khan said:

> "Should you have stirred those things
> that you chose to stir?
> Should you have touched those things
> that you chose to touch?
> Alas, the result is a nail
> in the cheek of my son!

My son is fighting for his life," he cried. "Let us attack!"

'But Achiq-shirun said: "Khan, Khan, don't do this! When we were seeking the longed-for son, we hung out the magic flags and chanted the magic words — *Abui, babui* — dearest, most dear! We prayed and sought for him: he was born, and now we must care for him. Most of the Mongols are with us. Jamuqa, Altan and Quchar are in our camp. Those who rebelled and joined Temujin, where can they go?

> They are
> riders with nothing but horses,
> shelterers with nothing but trees.

If they don't come back we will go and get them, gathering them up in our skirts like so much horse dung."

'The Ong Khan listened to Achiq-shirun and then he said: "You are right. The most important thing is my son. Look after him and see that he is not jolted on the road."

'Then he left and returned to the place where they had fought.'

All this Qada'an-daldurqan told Chinggis Khan.

After this Chinggis Khan moved downstream along the Qalqa river. Then he rounded up his soldiers and counted them. There were two thousand six hundred men. Chinggis took half of them and set off along the east bank of the river. The other half he sent up the east bank under the command of the

Uru'ut and Mangqut clans. They hunted for provisions as
they journeyed, and Quyildar, whose wound had not yet
healed and who had been warned by Chinggis not to exert
himself, ignored his chief and went to hunt the wild beasts. It
was too much for him: he collapsed and died. Chinggis buried
him on the Tilted cliffs, at Or-nu'u, on a curve in the Qalqa
river.

Then, knowing that Terge, Emel and other members of the
Onggirat were camped by the mouth of the Qalqa, where it
flows into Lake Buyur, Chinggis Khan sent Jurchedei and his
Uru'ut followers in search of them, saying:

'From the very beginning the Onggirat have depended

> on their daughters' complexions,
> on the colour of their cheeks.

They will either submit to us, or not, and if they don't we will
wage war on them.'

Jurchedei went off and the Onggirat immediately surrendered to him. As a result Chinggis Khan left them and their
possessions intact.

Having subdued the Onggirat, he moved on to pitch his
camp on the east bank of the Tungge stream. Then he sent
Arqai-qasar and Sugegei-je'un to the Ong Khan with a
message:

'Tell my father this: "I have pitched my camp on the east
side of the Tungge stream. The grass is good here, and our
geldings are growing strong." Then say: "My father, why do
you want to punish me? What is your grudge? If you had
wished to chastise your humble son, why did you not let him
sleep first? Here we are living in peace, yet you would cut the
legs from our beds and disturb the very smoke from our fires
as it curls upwards. Why do you punish us like this?" Tell the
khan my father:

> "By a man standing in the wings
> you have been needled,
> by a man coming at you sideways
> you have been provoked.

Don't you remember what we promised each other by Jorqal-
qun? Did we not say:

> If, by the teeth of a snake,
> we are bitten,
> let us resist the poison,
> let it not enter.
> Let us understand, by teeth, by mouth,
> and trust each other.

Did we not agree? My father, even as we parted we understood
each other:

> If by a snake's back teeth
> we are slandered,
> let us resist it,
> let it not enter.
> Let us understand, by mouth, by tongue,
> and trust each other.

Did we not say so? Even as we parted we understood each
other in word and deed. Look at me: I have only a few men
but I never asked you for more. I am humble, but I never
asked you for better men than I. On a cart with two shafts, if
one should break, the ox cannot pull it. Was I not your second
shaft? On a cart with two wheels, if one should break, the
cart cannot move. Was I not your second wheel? Think back
to earlier days. Your father made you khan, naming you the
eldest of his forty sons. Yet you killed two of your younger
brothers, and a third fled with his life to take refuge with the
Naiman people.

' "Don't you remember? Your uncle rode out against you
for killing your brothers. When you saw him coming you fled
for your life down the Selengge river with a hundred men,
and hid yourself in the Qara'un pass. Then, to curry favour
with the Merkit tribe, you gave your daughter to Tokto'a,
and you begged for help, saying, 'My uncle Gur Khan has
taken my people away from me.'

' "My own father came to your rescue then, bringing men
of the Tayyichi'ut to help him. They pursued Gur Khan from
the place of the Three Grasses to Qashin and got your people

back for you. You met by the Black forest on the Tu'ula river
and swore brotherhood together. You made a promise to my
father, saying:

' " 'You have done me great service, and I shall repay it to
your children's children. Let Heaven above and Earth below
decide our destiny.' That was what you said in your gratitude.

' "And afterwards Erge-qara begged soldiers from the
Naiman tribe to ride against you, and again you ran for your
life. But you left your people behind. With a handful of men
you threw yourself on the mercy of Gur Khan of the Qara-
kidat; yet within a year you had turned against him. You left
the lands of the Sarta'ul and wandered, suffering, through the
territories of the Uiqut and the Tangqut, your only meat and
drink the milk of five goats tethered in a line and the blood
of your camels. When you came to me you had nothing except
a blind yellow horse with a black mane and tail, and I took
you in, my father, because I remembered that in days gone by
you and my father had sworn brotherhood.

' "I sent messengers to meet you. I even went myself to
welcome you at the Guse'ur lake. When I saw that you were
suffering I raised levies for you; and because you had sworn
brotherhood with my father I became your son there in the
Black forest on the Tu'ula river.

' "Don't you remember? That winter I brought you to my
camp and looked after you until the summer had been and
gone. Then in the autumn I rode out against the Merkit people
and fought with Toqto'a at Stronghold ridge. I drove them
back towards the Burqujin lowlands and plundered them. I
took their herds, their palace-tents, their grain — all of it —
and gave it to you, my father. I did not let you hunger for
even half a day. I did not let you grow thin for even half a
month.

' "Don't you remember? We drove Buyiruq Khan of the
Guchugur across the Altai mountains and pursued him down
the Urunggu river until we could finish him off. As we
returned, we found our way blocked by Kokse'u-sabraq and
his Naiman soldiers. It was too late for fighting then, and we
agreed to wait until morning. Don't you remember? We spent
the night in battle formation and you lit fires for your soldiers.

' "But by morning you had gone, slipping away upstream along the Qara-se'ul river. We looked round next day and there was no sign of you. 'You have made a burnt offering of us,' said I, and I too moved on, crossing the Eder and Altai rivers where they meet.

' "I pitched my camp on the Sa'ari steppe. Then Kokse'u-sabraq went after you and stole Senggum's wife, his children, his people — everything he had. He plundered half your people, with their herds and all their belongings.

' "The sons of Toqto'a were there with their clans, but they turned their backs on you then and went off to join their father at Barqujin. You sent a message to me there. Don't you remember? You begged me to send my four best geldings to protect you from the Naiman. And (because I am not like you) I sent them — Bo'orchu, Muqali, Boro'ul and Chila'un-ba'atur — and I ordered my men to make themselves ready.

' "Senggum, meanwhile, was fighting at Hula'an-qut. His horse had been shot in the flank by an arrow and he was on the point of being captured. My best geldings arrived just in time. They rescued Senggum, your wives, your daughters, your people, your clan — all of them. You said it yourself: 'By sending his best geldings, my son Temujin has saved my scattered people for me.'

' "Now, my father, tell me: why have I deserved this punishment? Send me word by Qulbari-quri and Idurgen; or, if not both, then send at least the latter." '

When the Ong Khan heard this message he said: 'Oh my poor son. If I part with him I must part with my honour. If I part with him I must part with my duty.' And he suffered in his heart, and swore an oath, saying:

'If when I see my son I am disappointed, let my blood be shed like this... ' and he pierced the inner edge of his little finger with the knife he used to trim his arrows, and as the blood flowed he caught it in a small birch-bark container.

'Give this to my son,' he commanded.

Chinggis Khan also sent a messenger to his sworn brother Jamuqa:

'Because you have tired of me you have caused a rift between me and my father the khan. In the old days, whichever of us rose first was allowed to drink from my father's blue cup. As I always rose first, I drank from his cup and you were jealous of me. Now you can drink from his blue cup to your heart's content, and much good may it do you!'

Then Chinggis Khan sent a message to Altan and Quchar: 'You have both forsaken me. Did you intend to abandon me openly, or were you going to do it in secret? Quchar, when I told you that as the son of Nekun-taishi you should become khan, you were not willing to do it. Altan, when I said you should become khan and govern like your father, Qutula, before you, you were not willing to do it. And when I said to Sacha and Taichu: "You are older than we are and should become khans," they would not be persuaded. I said that you should all become khans but none of you were willing. Instead you said: "You be our khan"; so I did as I was told and governed. Had you become khans I would have ridden out as a scout against your enemies. If Heaven had protected me I should have plundered your enemies for you.

> I would have brought
> women and maids with beautiful cheeks,
> geldings with fine rumps,
> and given them to you.
> I would have rounded up
> the wily beasts and the beasts of the rock
> and, squeezing their forelegs together,
> brought them to you.
> For you I would have squeezed
> the thighs of the beasts of the cliff,
> for you I would have squeezed
> the bellies of the beasts of the steppe.
> All this would I have done.

So now be good companions to the khan my father. Shall it be said that you tire so easily of your chiefs? At least let it not be said that I have made you what you are! And let no one pitch their camp at the source of the Three Rivers!'*

* The Kerulen, the Tu'ula and the Onon.

Chinggis also sent a messenger to To'oril, calling him 'younger brother', and saying:

'Once upon a time Tumbinai and Charaqa-lingqu captured a slave named Oqda. And the son of Oqda was the slave Subegei. And the son of Subegei was Kokochu-kirsa'an, and his son was Yegei-qongtaqar. You, To'oril, are the son of Yegei-qongtaqar, yet you stride around, flattering the Ong Khan as if you had people to pledge to him. My people will not be governed so, nor Altan and Quchar. I call you "younger brother" because you are

> my great-great-grandfather's
> threshold slave,
> and the personal slave
> of my great-grandfather's door.

That is my message to To'oril.'

Then Chinggis sent a message to his sworn brother Senggum, saying:

'I am the son that came ready clothed,* while you were born naked – yet our father the khan cared for us both as equals. Sworn brother, you were jealous of me, afraid that I would come between you and the Ong Khan your father. So you drove me out. Do not worry the heart of our father day and night any more, but comfort him as you come and go. You cannot forgo your old ambition — while the khan your father lives you intend to be khan, and you worry his heart with your vaunting. I tell you, you should not give him such pain! Send emissaries to me, my sworn brother, and let those emissaries include Bilge-beki and Todo-en.'

And he sent a further message, saying: 'When you send your emissaries, let the khan our father send two, and you, my sworn brother, two. Let Jamuqa send two more, and Altan, Quchar and Achiq-shirun two each.'

These words he sent by Arqai-qasar and Sugegei-je'un; and when they had repeated them, Senggum said:

'When did he ever call the Ong Khan father? Why doesn't he call him "the old slaughterer" instead? And when did he

---

* i.e. he was adopted.

ever call me "sworn brother"? Didn't he always say that I
stuck to Toqto'a the Shaman like the tail of one of his sheep,
waiting for a chance to oust my father? I know what his
riddling means — these are the first words of war! Bilge-beki
and Todo-en, hoist the banner and fatten the geldings! There's
no time to lose!'

So Arqai-qasar went back to Chinggis Khan, but Sugegei-
je'un stayed behind because his wife and children were there
with To'oril and he was afraid to leave them.

Arqai related Senggum's words to Chinggis, and soon afterwards they moved on and pitched their camp at the Baljuna
lake. There they came across the Qorulas of Cho'os-chaqan,
but the Qorulas submitted to Chinggis without a fight.

Then the Muslim Asan appeared mounted on a white camel.
He had come from Alaqush-digit-quri,* leader of the Onggut,
and was driving a thousand sheep downstream to barter for
sable and squirrel skins. He met Chinggis Khan as he stopped
to water his animals at the Baljuna lake. Chinggis was also
watering his animals when Qasar decided to abandon his wife
and children to the Ong Khan and make his way to join his
chief. With a few companions he crossed the ridges of the
Qara'un-jidun, but at first could not find him. He and his
friends suffered hardship, eating hide and sinews, before
they eventually caught up with Chinggis at Baljuna. Chinggis
rejoiced to see them, and decided to send a message there and
then to the Ong Khan. After consulting Qasar, he sent word
through Qali-udar of the Jewuret and Chaqurqan of the
Uriangqad, saying:

'I looked for my elder brother, but he had disappeared. I
looked for his tracks but I could not find them. I shouted for
him, but my voice could not be heard. Now I am lying on
the ground, a lump of earth for my pillow, gazing at the
stars. My wife and children are with the khan my father.
If my trusted man will come to me, I will go to the khan my
father.'

Chinggis said: 'Give him this message and say it comes
from Qasar. Tell him that Qasar says they should move

* His name means 'bird of many colours', or magpie.

immediately and meet at Arqal-geugi on the Kerulen river. There they must come.'

They agreed on the message and sent the emissaries off. Then Chinggis Khan ordered Jurchedei and Arqai to go ahead as scouts, and, following closely on their heels with his own men, he soon arrived at Arqal-geugi.

Qali'udar and Chaqurqan meanwhile had reached the Ong Khan and delivered the message, saying that it came from Qasar.

The Ong Khan had had his gold-painted, latticed yurt* erected and was feasting unconcernedly when they arrived. His only answer was: 'If that's so, let Qasar come.' And he added: 'We will send Iturgen. He can be trusted.'

So Iturgen was sent to the rendezvous, and there he saw a great army spread out. Turning tail, he fled. Qali'udar rode after him and because his horse was swift soon caught up with him, but he was afraid to take him prisoner. Instead he slowed him down by swerving first in front of him and then behind. Chaqurqan's horse was slow, but even from the fur-thest point of an arrow's flight he was able to hit Iturgen's black gelding in the rump and bring it down. They captured Iturgen and brought him back to camp. Chinggis said not a word to him. 'Take him to Qasar,' he decreed. 'Let Qasar decide his fate.' They took him to Qasar, who did not speak to him either, but cut him down on the spot and kicked his body aside.

Then Qali'udar and Chaqurqan reported back to Chinggis Khan. 'The Ong Khan was unconcerned,' they said. 'He had erected his gold-painted yurt and was feasting. Quick! We should take fresh horses, ride by night and take them by surprise!'

Chinggis approved their plan and swiftly sent Jurchedei and Arqai ahead as scouts. They travelled by night until they reached the Jer-qabchiqay pass on the Jeje'er heights. There they found the Ong Khan's camp and surrounded it. For three days and three nights they fought and on the third day the

---

* A latticed yurt consisted of a collapsible trellised frame over which sheets of felt were fitted.

Ong Khan's men surrendered, exhausted. How the Ong Khan and Senggum managed to escape no one knows. One of their leaders, Qadaq-ba'atur of the Jirgin, came to surrender, saying:

'We have fought for three nights and three days, and all the time I thought: "How can I let my rightful khan be captured and killed?" I could not forsake him. I fought and battled to rid him of his enemies and save his life. If you kill me now, I will accept my fate, but if Chinggis Khan should choose to favour me, I will serve him well.'

Chinggis approved of Qadaq-ba'atur's words. 'He could not forsake his khan,' he said. 'Did he not fight to rid him of his enemies and save his life? This man is a worthy companion.' With this decree he showed him favour and did not have him killed.

Then he said: 'Because Quyildar gave his life for me, Qadaq-ba'atur and a hundred of the Jirgin tribe will serve Quyildar's wife and children. If any sons are born to them they will serve the seed of Quyildar's family. If daughters are born they shall not be betrothed as their parents wish, but shall serve as Quyildar's wife and children shall desire.'

This was his decree. Quyildar had committed his children to Chinggis's care in case he was killed in battle, and Chinggis kept his word. 'Because Quyildar served me, his descendants shall receive an orphan's recompense,' he said. So it was done.

CHAPTER SEVEN

The Ong Khan's death. The bragging of Tayang Khan. The battle with the Naiman people.

SO IT WAS THAT THE KEREYIT CLAN WAS DEFEATED.
Chinggis Khan distributed its people here and there as favours.
Taqai-ba'atur of the Suldud got a hundred members of the
Jirgin tribe as a reward for his services.

Then Chinggis Khan issued a decree: the Ong Khan's younger brother, Jaqa-gambu, had two daughters. The elder,
Ibaqa-beki, he took for himself, and he gave the younger one,
Sorqaqtani-beki, to his youngest son, Tolui. As a result of this
he kept the members of Jaqa-gambu's family together, saying:
'Jaqa-gambu is the second shaft of my cart. I shall show him
favour and not disperse his people.'

Then Chinggis Khan issued another decree: 'Let Badai and
Kishiliq have the Ong Khan's gold-painted tent, his golden
kumiss bowl, his cups, his containers, his servants and his
people as a reward for their service. Even the Ongqojit-kereyit
duty-men shall be theirs. They shall carry quivers and drink
the ceremonial wine, and the seed of their seed shall be free
men forever. If they gallop in pursuit of many enemies, the
plunder shall be theirs. If they kill many wild beasts, they
shall keep what they kill.'

This was his decree, and he followed it with another: 'Badai
and Kishiliq were for me the difference between life and
death: the Almighty Spirits of Eternal Heaven decreed that
the Kereyit people should be brought down and that I should
be raised to the high throne. Let the seed of my seed, who
will one day sit upon that throne, never forget the men who
have served them.'

Then they plundered the Kereyit tribe, and dispersed the
people among themselves, so nobody went short. They shared
out the Tumen-tubegen as well, and by the end of the day the
Olon-dongqoyit had also been divided between them. The

Jirgin ringleaders, those bloody thieves, they hacked to pieces, so there were not enough Jirgin slaves to go round.

They spent the winter at Abji'a-kodeger. The Ong Khan and Senggum, meanwhile, had left their people to their fate, and run away. The Ong Khan was soon thirsty, and ventured down to the Nekun water to drink. But the Naiman's watchman, Qori-subechi, the 'watcher of the pass', captured the Ong Khan, and though the Ong Khan told him who he was, the watchman didn't believe him: he killed him on the spot.

Senggum did not go down to the water with his father, but skirted round it and found himself in the Chol desert. There, while he was looking for water, he saw some wild asses which had been bitten by gnats. Senggum dismounted, and approached them stealthily. His equerry, Kokochu, and Kokochu's wife were with him, and Senggum gave the man his horse to hold; but as soon as he had taken the gelding's halter, Kokochu turned round and trotted back the way he had come. His wife called after him:

'When he spread out the golden cloth and set a feast upon it, he called you "my Kokochu". How can you forsake your own khan like this, deserting him, tossing him aside?'

Kokochu said: 'You sound as if you want Senggum for a husband.'

His wife replied: 'I've always been told that it was women who were as two-faced as dogs; at least leave me Senggum's golden cup so that I can give him water to drink.'

Kokochu threw the cup down behind him. 'Take it!' he said, and trotted away.

After a while Kokochu came to Chinggis Khan's camp. He said: 'I have left Senggum in the desert and have come to join you,' and he told Chinggis exactly what had happened.

Then Chinggis said: 'Kokochu's wife deserves my favour; but who can trust a man like this who deserts his rightful khan?' And he cut him down, throwing his body aside.

Meanwhile Gurbesu, nicknamed 'the Lizard', who was the mother of Tayang Khan of the Naiman tribe, said: 'The Ong Khan used to be a great man. Bring in his head, and if it is truly him, we will make an offering to it.'

She sent an emissary to Qori-subechi and had him cut off the head and bring it to her. As soon as she saw it she recognised the great khan himself, and placed it on a white felt carpet. Then she commanded her daughters-in-law to perform their ceremonial duties: wine was poured and the Mongolian fiddle was played.

Holding her cup on high, she offered it to the head, and the head acknowledged her offering and smiled. 'It smiled!' cried Tayang Khan, and immediately he trampled it to pieces.

Up spoke Kokse'u-sabraq: 'You wanted the Ong Khan's head to be brought to you, yet you have trampled it to pieces. How can you justify such dishonourable behaviour? Our own dogs are beginning to bark without good reason. It is an evil omen. Did not Inancha-bilge Khan say: "My wife is young and I am getting old. My son Tayang was only born because of my prayers, and, alas, he was born lazy. Will he ever be able to govern all my many different people with their many evil qualities, I wonder?" Now you can hear the barking of the dogs getting closer, and you can see the rule of Gurbesu, our queen, becoming harsh. You are soft, Tayang Khan. You don't know about anything except hunting and falconry.'

And he rebuked Tayang.

Then Tayang answered and said: 'I've been told there are a few Mongols in the east. In former days they frightened the great old khan with their quivers. They forced him to rebel against them, and he died. Perhaps they would like to be khan like him? The sun and the moon shine brightly in the same Heaven — so be it. Let them both shine. But here on Earth there's no room for more than one great khan. I say we should go and take those Mongols!'

At this his mother Gurbesu spoke: 'And what will you do with them?' she said. 'They smell appalling and their clothes are filthy. They live a long way away. I should leave them there. But why not bring their neat daughters-in-law, their fine girls, to us? We will make them wash their hands and feet, and perhaps they will milk our cows and sheep for us.'

Then Tayang Khan said: 'So what is stopping us? Let's go after those Mongols and take away their quivers.'

Kokse'u-sabraq answered him: 'Oh, you use such big

words. Is this right, you lazy khan? You should keep such words to yourself.'

But Tayang would not be warned. He sent an emissary, Torbi-tash, to Alaqush-digit-quri of the Onggut, saying: 'I've been told there are a few Mongols in the east. If you attack from the right flank, I'll attack from here, and together we'll take away those Mongols' quivers.'

This was the message he sent.

Alaqush replied at once: 'I cannot become your right hand in this,' he declared, and at the same time he sent a message to Chinggis Khan, saying: 'Tayang Khan is on the march to take your quivers. He asked me to be his right hand, but I refused, and now I am sending you this warning, for fear he will take your quivers from you.'

When Alaqush's messenger reached Chinggis Khan he was out hunting on the Teme'en steppe. As they encircled Tulkin-che'ud they discussed what they should do. Many of the soldiers said: 'What can we do? Our geldings are lean.' But Otchigui-noyan was more robust: 'You say your geldings are lean. How can you be so feeble? My geldings are fat. Why do we sit here and listen to such talk?'

Belgutei-noyan backed him up. 'What's the good of being alive if our quivers have been snatched by the enemy? Better a man should lay down his bones with his bow and quiver. The Naiman brag about the size of their nation. For that reason alone we should ride out against them. Do we really think we shall have any difficulty in taking their quivers? Won't we see them leaving their herds behind? Won't we see them leaving their palace-tents, while their people scuttle off to take refuge in the high places? To be sure, their words are very grand. We should ride out against them at once.'

Chinggis Khan approved of Belgutei's words, and when they returned from hunting they immediately moved out and set up their camp at the Tilted cliffs on the Qalqa river.

There they counted their men and divided them into units of a thousand. Chinggis appointed leaders for every thousand men, and then for every hundred, and then for every group of ten. He also appointed six commanders-in-chief, Dodai-cherbi, Doqolqu-cherbi, Ogele-cherbi, Tolun-cherbi, Bucharan-cherbi and Soyiketu-cherbi; and when all this was done he chose eighty night-guards and seventy sentries and sent them forward to their posts in shifts. For this task he chose those who were skilful, with strong, handsome bodies.

Then he issued a decree, bestowing particular favour on Arqai-qasar: 'He shall choose heroes for a special unit of one thousand men, and they shall be ranged in front of me and do battle on my behalf. On the days when there is no fighting, they will form my bodyguard and will work in shifts to protect me.'

Finally he decreed that Ogele-cherbi should command the seventy sentries, in consultation with Qudus-qalchan.

Then Chinggis Khan gave his orders:

'The quiver-bearers, sentries, cooks, door-keepers and equerries will go to their posts for the day shift. Before the sun sets the night-guards must take over and look after the geldings. The guards must ensure that those who should be on guard outside my door are on their feet, while those who are resting should squat down next to my yurt. While we are eating our early morning soup, the quiver-bearers and sentries will report to the night-guards. Along with the cooks and the door-keepers they will be assigned to specific posts with specific duties to perform. Each period of duty shall last three days and nights, and after three days' leave those on the night shift will change to the day shift, and those on the day shift will become night-guards and spend the night outside my yurt.'

In this way Chinggis organised his units of a thousand men, appointed his commanders, and posted his sentries and his night-guards. A thousand heroes were chosen for his own special unit, and then, from the Tilted cliffs on the Qalqa river, he rode out against the Naiman people.

In the Year of the Rat, 1204, on the sixteenth day of the fourth lunar month, Chinggis Khan made his oblations to the banner and rode upstream along the Kerulen river. He sent Jebe and Qubilai ahead as scouts, and when they reached the Sa'ari steppe they saw the Naiman look-outs were already there, on the peak of Mount Kangqarqan.

There was a scuffle between the look-outs on both sides, in the course of which the Naiman snatched one of our horses — an off-white gelding with an inferior saddle. The look-outs were not impressed. 'Those Mongol horses are lean,' they said.

When our troops reached the Sa'ari steppe they halted and discussed what to do next.

Dodai-cherbi said to Chinggis Khan: 'There are only a few of us, and, what's more, we are tired after our journey. We should wait until our geldings have had a chance to graze and fatten. If we pitch our camp here, spreading ourselves out over the steppe and lighting five fires each as far apart as possible, we might scare the Naiman. Their army is bigger than ours, but their khan is said to be a weakling who never leaves his yurt. Our fires should keep the Naiman at bay until our geldings have had a chance to get fat; then we will bear down on their look-outs and drive them back towards the main body of their army. With luck we can take advantage of the confusion and do battle with them.'

Chinggis Khan approved of Dodai-cherbi's plan. He sent out the order for the able-bodied to light the fires, giving exact instructions as to how it should be done. The soldiers pitched their camp and lit five fires each, as far apart as they possibly could. That night the Naiman look-outs saw the fires from the top of the mountain and said to each other: 'I thought we agreed that the Mongols were few! There are more fires out there than stars.'

They had already sent the off-white horse with the inferior saddle to Tayang Khan, and now they sent a message to him, saying: 'The Mongols have pitched their tents all over the Sa'ari steppe. Day by day more of them appear, swarming all over the steppe, and there are now more fires than stars!'

Tayang Khan had stayed by the Qachir water. As soon as he heard the message he sent word to his son Guchuluk, the Mighty Khan.

'The Mongol geldings are lean,' he said, 'but our look-outs have seen more fires than stars out there on the steppe, so their army must be vast.

> If we do battle in earnest,
> won't it be hard to draw back?
> If we do battle in earnest,
> they will not blink their black eyes,
> they will not shrink
> though their cheeks are pierced
> and their black blood flows.
> What will become of us
> at the hands of these hardy Mongols,
> if we do battle in earnest?

It is said that their horses are lean. Let us gather up our people and move out. We will cross the Altai mountains, reorganising our troops as we go and luring the enemy after us until we reach the southern slopes. Then we will give them a dog's fight! We will turn and fall on them! Our horses are fat. As their horses tire, ours will become fit — then we can turn and attack them.'

This was the message he sent to his son; but Guchuluk said: 'That woman Tayang! His heart has failed him again. Where do all these Mongols come from? Most of the tribes are already on our side, along with Jamuqa. Tayang is nothing but

> a pregnant woman
> who dare not move
> beyond her pissing place,
> a tethered calf
> who dare not move
> beyond her pasture.

That's why his heart fails him and he sends us such weasel words.'

Then he sent a message to his father through an emissary, calling him womanish.

Tayang was pained and hurt by his son's words, and replied: 'My son Guchuluk is powerful and proud. I hope his arrogance will not desert him in the face of the enemy and death. Once we close with them it will be too late to draw back.'

To these words Qori-subechi, one of Tayang's great commanders, answered:

'Inancha-bilge Khan, your father, never showed a man's back or a horse's rump to any enemy. How can your heart fail you now, so early in this enterprise? We should have brought your mother instead and put her in charge of the army. The pity is that Kokse'u-sabraq is old, and our soldiers have become lax. The Mongols have fortune on their side now, but not we. You are lazy, Tayang, and you have failed us.'

And slapping his quiver, he turned his back on his khan and trotted off.

At this Tayang became very angry. 'A dying life, a suffering body — they are common to all men. So be it. We will fight.'

He moved downstream from the Qachir water along the Tamir river, and, crossing the Orqon river, he skirted the foot of Naqu-kun mountain until he reached Chakir-ma'ut. Chinggis Khan's look-outs saw him approaching and reported back to their chief, saying: 'The Naiman are coming.'

Then Chinggis issued a decree: 'They are many and will lose many. We are few and will lose few!' And so saying he rode straight out against their advance guard and routed them.

Then he and his captains decided to press the attack, and they agreed the following plan: they would move forward in 'bush-clump' formation — small groups of soldiers keeping a low profile but always keeping in contact with each other: when they faced the enemy they would line up in 'lake array' for the attack, sending waves of men to surround and contain the foe: finally they would strike at the very centre using the 'chisel attack', with lines of soldiers penetrating the heart of the enemy in hand-to-hand combat.

Chinggis took up his position in the vanguard. Qasar he put in charge of the main army, while Otchigin-noyan took over the reserve horse.

In the meantime the Naiman army withdrew from Chakir-ma'ut and lined up on the southern side of Naqu-kun, along the foot of the mountain. Our advance guard had already engaged theirs and had driven them back so that they were forced to rejoin the main body of their troops. Tayang Khan saw their flight, and questioned Jamuqa, who had come with his own troops to swell the Naiman attack.

'Who are those wolves', he asked, 'chasing our sheep back into their pen? What men are they?'

And Jamuqa answered:

'My sworn brother Temujin has four warriors who were raised, like hounds, on human flesh. They have been kept on chains, but now he has released them to harry your look-outs.

> Those four hounds have
> cast copper foreheads,
> snouts like chisels,
> tongues like awls.
> With iron hearts
> and whips for swords,
> eating the dew
> and riding the wind they go.
> On killing days
> their food is human flesh,
> on battle days
> their food is human flesh.

They have been chained, suppressed and tethered. Now they have slipped the leash, and, slavering with joy, they come after us. You want to know who those four hounds are?' continued Jamuqa. 'They are Jebe and Qubilai, Jelme and Sube'etei — those four.'

Then Tayang Khan said: 'Let us retreat a little and take a proper look at these barbarians.'

So they moved back up the mountain, until they stood astride its peak. Below them they could see Chinggis's hounds coming on fast, riding circles in their joy. Tayang Khan said again:

'What kind of men are these that caper like foals in the early morning, dancing for joy and sucking their mother's milk? Why are they circling like that?'

And Jamuqa answered:

> 'They chase men with spears,
> they chase the bloody bandits

> and men with swords;
> they kill them and cast them down.
> The names of these plunderers?
> The Uru'ut, the Mangqut tribes.

Why shouldn't they be happy, now they are so close to us?'

At this Tayang Khan said: 'If that's the case, we should keep our distance from these barbarians.'

So they climbed a higher mountain and stood there watching.

'There is someone behind them,' observed Tayang Khan; 'a man leads their army, slavering like a starved falcon. Who is he?'

And Jamuqa replied:

'That is my sworn brother Temujin. His body

> is smelted from cast copper;
> there's no crack for an awl to pierce.
> It is forged from wrought iron;
> there's no crack for a needle to pierce.

Do you see how Temujin comes after you, slavering like a starved falcon? Didn't you Naimans say that once you had laid eyes on the Mongols you would leave them without the skin of a kid's hoof to their name? Look at them now.'

Tayang Khan mused: 'This could be very awkward. We'd better go further up the mountain and stay there.'

So they climbed higher up the mountain, and Tayang Khan asked Jamuqa: 'Who are all those people following Temujin?'

And Jamuqa replied:

'Mother Ho'elun nourished one of her sons on human flesh.

> His body is three fathoms high,
> he eats like an ox, a three-year-old,
> he wears three layers of armour
> and three bulls draw his chariot.
> If he swallows a man whole
> complete with quiver,
> his throat will not even be bruised;
> he can swallow a man
> and not be satisfied.

> In anger he draws his bow
> and lets his two-pronged arrow fly;
> it pierces ten or twenty men
> on the far side of the mountain.
> In anger he draws his bow
> and lets his iron dart fly;
> it pierces his enemies
> on the far side of the steppe.
> When he draws his bow to the full
> and lets his arrows fly,
> they cover nine hundred fathoms;
> when he half-draws his bow
> and lets his arrows fly,
> he covers five hundred fathoms.
> He was born a man like no other,
> a monster, lizard-like:
> his name is Jochi-qasar.

That's who he is!'

Then Tayang Khan said: 'If that is the case we must struggle even further up to the mountain's peak.'

So they climbed further up and there they watched. And Tayang Khan said again: 'Who is the man behind him?'

And Jamuqa replied:

'That is Mother Ho'elun's youngest son, Otchigin. They say he's friendly, that he goes to bed early and gets up late,

> yet he does not linger far behind the soldiers,
> he does not stay in the rearguard of the battle.'

Tayang Khan said: 'If that is the case, we should go to the very summit of the mountain.'

But after Jamuqa had finished what he had to say to Tayang Khan he distanced himself from the Naiman tribe, and, as soon as he could, he sent a message to Chinggis Khan.

'Tell my sworn brother this,' he said. 'Tayang Khan is scared to death after what I have told him. Terrified, he has struggled and climbed; frightened of being killed, he has taken himself to the top of the mountain. Now, my sworn brother, take courage. They are in retreat up the mountain and will not dare to face you. As for myself, I've left them to their fate.'

It was late in the day and the sun was setting when Chinggis Khan and his men surrounded the Naqu-kun mountain. They spent the night on their feet, waiting for dawn. Meanwhile the Naiman tried to escape, but in the dark they fell and rolled down the mountainside, piling on top of one another. Their bones were smashed and their bodies were cut to pieces —they were crushed to death like so many rotten logs.

The following day Chinggis Khan found Tayang Khan and finished him off. His son Guchuluk, meanwhile, was camped elsewhere. He took the few men he had with him and tried to retreat. He was almost caught by the Tamir river, but he gave Chinggis's men the slip and got away. There on the southern side of the Altai mountain Chinggis Khan defeated the Naiman nation and subjugated it. The tribes who had allied themselves with Jamuqa, including the Tayyichi'ut and the Onggirat, also submitted to him there. Chinggis had Tayang's mother, Gurbesu, brought before him. 'I thought you said the Mongols stank,' he mocked her, 'so what are you doing here now?' Then he made her his wife.

In the autumn of the same year, Chinggis Khan fought Toqto'a-beki of the Merkit at the source of the Qaradal river. He forced Toqto'a to retreat and out there on the Sa'ari steppe he plundered his kinsmen, his tribesmen and his kingdom. Toqto'a, his two sons, and a handful of followers were lucky to escape with their lives, but the Merkit were comprehensively plundered.

Meanwhile Dayyir-usun, who belonged to the Qo'as branch of the Merkit tribe, decided to take his own daughter to present to Chinggis Khan. On the way he was stopped by a group of soldiers, and, seeing Naya'a-noyan of the Ba'arit among them, Dayyir-usun spoke to him. 'I want to present my daughter to Chinggis Khan,' he said, 'so I'm taking this road.'

Then Naya'a-noyan said: 'We'd better go together.' And while they waited he explained: 'If you go by yourselves in these confused times the soldiers you meet will almost certainly kill you, and your daughter will suffer in consequence.'

He made them wait for three days and three nights, then he himself accompanied them to Chinggis Khan.

At first Chinggis was angry on principle. He questioned Naya'a rigorously and severely about the delay. 'Why did you hold them up, Naya'a? What was the reason for it?'

But Dayyir-usun's daughter spoke on his behalf: 'Naya'a told us he was one of your great lords. He said he would travel with us to protect us from the disorderly bands of soldiers on the road. He wanted to make sure I was brought to you safely, so he warned us of the danger. Now, if we had not met him, we might have run into soldiers on the way, and in the confusion there's no telling what they would have done to us. Perhaps we were lucky to meet Naya'a. Before the khan questions him further, perhaps he will favour me by inspecting this body, born by Heaven's destiny to my father and my mother.'

So she spoke, and her petition was laid before the khan.

While he was being questioned Naya'a said: 'I will never turn my face from my khan towards anyone.

> Foreign girls and women
> with bright complexions,
> geldings with fine rumps,
> when I encounter them
> I say: "They are my khan's."

If my desire ever strays, then let me die.'

Chinggis Khan approved of Lady Qulan's petition. On that very day he proved her words on her body, and found that it was as she had said. So he showed her his favour and loved her. He found Naya'a honest too, and favoured him. 'He is a man who speaks the truth,' declared Chinggis Khan. 'I shall command great deeds of him, and I shall favour him.'

CHAPTER EIGHT

The destruction of the Merkit tribe. Chinggis becomes Great Khan, organises the Mongol people and dispenses favours.

AFTER HE HAD PLUNDERED THE MERKIT TRIBE, Chinggis Khan took Doregene, one of the wives belonging to Toqto'a's eldest son Qudu, and gave her to Ogodei Khan. In the meantime half the Merkit tribe rebelled and built a barricade against Chinggis's soldiers. Chinggis immediately gave orders to Sorqan-shira's son, Chimbai, to mount an attack on the barricade. In the ensuing mêlée, Toqto'a and his two sons, Qudu and Chila'un, together with a few of their men, turned their backs on their own men and narrowly escaped with their lives. Chinggis went after them, spending the winter on the southern side of the Altai mountains.

Then in the spring of the Year of the Ox (1205) he crossed the Altai, but Guchuluk, whose Naiman clan had already been defeated, rebelled, and, with a few loyal men, went to join Toqto'a of the Merkit. They met at Buqdurma and lined up their troops ready to attack Chinggis's army. As soon as Chinggis arrived they fought, and there Toqto'a fell, brought down by a stray arrow. His sons could not bury him, nor could they take his body with them, so they cut off his head and took that away instead.

But even the Merkit and Naiman tribes together could not stop Chinggis Khan. They were forced to retreat across the Erdish river where most of them were drowned. A few managed to reach the far bank, where they split up and went their way. Guchuluk wandered through Ui'urtai and Qarlu'ut territory before joining up with the Gur Khan of the Qarakitat, who was camped by the Chui river in the land of Sarda'ul. Toqto'a's sons, meanwhile, with the remnant of their band, found themselves in the lands of the Kanglin and

Kimcha'ut. From thence came Chinggis Khan, back across the Altai to his base camp. By then Chimbai had overcome the Merkit barricade and Chinggis was able to issue the following decree: 'We had already killed those who deserved death, and those who were left had been divided up among our soldiers.'

Once again the Merkit, though they had already submitted, had rebelled at the base camp, and had had to be put down. 'I said that I would let them stay together as a tribe,' said Chinggis, 'but they have rebelled against me.'

So the Merkit were dispersed there and then in all directions until the tribe ceased to exist.

In that same Year of the Ox Chinggis Khan commanded: 'Let Sube'etei pursue the sons of Toqto'a in a waggon reinforced with iron.'

And he gave Sube'etei this message:

'Toqto'a's sons were frightened of us. They ran away. We shot at each other, but they ran like wild asses with lassos round their necks, or deer with arrows in their flesh. If they grew wings and flew up to the heavens, would you, Sube'etei, turn into a gerfalcon and fly after them? If they burrowed with their nails like marmots into the ground, would you become the iron bar that rooted them out? If they became fish and swam towards the Tenggis ocean, would you be able to turn into a game-net, large or small, to scoop them out of the sea? Sube'etei, I'm sending you out once more to climb high passes and ford deep rivers. You are going to distant lands: look after your soldiers' horses, don't let them become too lean; eke out your provisions, don't let them become too scarce. If a horse gets too thin there's no saving it; if you run out of provisions, you'll have nothing left to share. Think ahead. You'll see plenty of wild beasts on your journey, but don't let your soldiers gallop about, hunting promiscuously. If you want to supplement your provisions, send them out hunting in small bands to kill only what you need. Apart from that, let your men ride with the bit free; don't let them harness the saddle or tighten the bridle — that way they won't be able to gallop at will. Give your orders, and if anyone disobeys you have them rounded up and beaten. If anyone known to us transgresses, let him be sent back to me — make him come! Those whom we don't know, let them be executed on the spot.

> Beyond the rivers
> you will be beyond us.
> Stick to your principles.
> Beyond the mountains
> you will be parted from us.
> Think of nothing but your quest.

And if, by your strength and might, increased by the powers of the Almighty Spirits, you lay your hands on the sons of Toqto'a, don't bring them back to me. What's the good of that? Get rid of them there and then.'

That was his decree, and he added: 'I'm sending you out hunting now because when I was young I was frightened by the Three Merkit as they circled Burqan-qaldun three times. Now my sworn enemies are on the move again, swearing oaths against me with their mouths and tongues. You must penetrate the furthest lands and the deepest seas. You must pursue them to the end in the iron waggon I have made for you. In this Year of the Ox I am sending you into battle. If we are behind you, imagine we are facing you; if we are far away, imagine we are by your side. Then the Almighty Spirits will protect you.'

In 1205, when Chinggis Khan had completely crushed the Naiman and Merkit tribes, Jamuqa saw the last of his people taken from him. Left with only five companions, he became a thief, climbing the Tangnu mountains and killing a sheep which he and his men roasted and ate. And as they ate Jamuqa observed:

'Who else's son will be killing wild sheep to roast and eat like this?'

But while they ate the wild sheep's meat, Jamuqa's companions laid hands on their leader and dragged him before Chinggis Khan. Jamuqa, finding himself delivered into cap-

tivity by his own men, found someone to plead his cause to
his sworn brother, saying:

> 'These days black crows
> capture the mandarin duck;
> these days slaves and commoners
> lay hands on their own chief.
> How can you be taken in by that?
> These days brown buzzards
> carry off the male and female duck;
> these days slaves and slave-girls
> capture their rightful lord,
> attack him and cut him down...
> Oh, my wise brother,
> how can you be taken in by that?'

Chinggis answered these words with a decree:

'How can I let men live who have raised their hands against
their rightful lord? Men like that are fit companions for no
one. Let those who have raised their hands against their
rightful lord be executed forthwith, they and all their kinsmen.' And there, on the spot, in front of Jamuqa, he ordered
the execution of those who had laid hands on him.

Then Chinggis said: 'Tell Jamuqa this: "Now that we are
joined together, let us be friends at last. If we were two shafts
of the same cart, would you try to part from me? Now we
are united once more we should

> remind each other
> of things we have forgotten,
> wake each other
> from long sleep.
> Even when you left
> and lived apart,
> you were my brother,
> the blessed, the lucky one.
> Surely in the killing days
> you ached for me in your heart,
> in the pit of your stomach?
> Surely in the slaying days

you ached for me
in your heart and in your breast?
And if you ask me when
I knew the truth —
I knew when I fought
the Kereyit people
on the Qalaqaljit sands,
and you alerted me
to the words you had spoken
to the Ong Khan my father.

You showed me loyalty when you sent me that message, and
again when you sent me word about the Naiman tribe, saying:

'You killed them with your words,
you killed them with your mouth,
you taught me that to be afraid
was no better than being dead.'

That was your service to me."'

After Chinggis Khan had finished speaking, Jamuqa said:

'In earlier days when we were young, I agreed to be my
khan's sworn brother, to swear brotherhood in the Qorqonaq
forest. Together we drank the gold dust which can never
be digested and spoke the words which should never be
forgotten.

We shared a single quilt
and slept beneath it;
yet we were provoked
by one who came between us;
we were goaded
by one who slid in from the flank.
Thus we were parted.
I told myself the breach was serious.
Afraid that my black face
would be flayed off with shame,
unable to come close to you,
unable to look upon the kind face
of my sworn brother, my khan,
I left.

> I told myself the breach was serious;
> words had been spoken
> that could not be forgotten.
> Afraid that my red face
> would be peeled off with shame,
> unable to look at the true face
> of my sworn brother, the eagle-eyed,
> I left.

Now my sworn brother favours me and says: "Let us be friends again." But when it was right for us to be friends I was not your friend. Now, my sworn brother:

> you have pacified our peoples,
> you have unified our peoples.

Natives and foreigners, they have raised you to the throne of khan. The world awaits you. What's the use now of my being your friend? On the contrary, in the black night I would haunt your dreams, in the bright day I would trouble your heart.

> I would be the louse in your cellar,
> the splinter in your door panel.
> My paternal grandmothers were useless,
> and I, my thoughts exalted above my brother,
> made a mistake.

Now, my sworn brother, look at our two lives. My name rose with the sun and sets with the sun; but you, sworn brother, had a wiser mother and a hero's birth. Your younger brothers were skilful, and the seventy-three geldings — your warrior companions — were powerful. I was overwhelmed. My mother and father I lost when I was small and I have no younger brothers. My wife is a gossip and I have no trusted friends. My sworn brother was destined by Heaven and he has over-whelmed me. If you truly favour me, you will kill me now, without shedding my blood — kill me, and lay my bones to rest on the high ground. Then, eternally and forever, I will protect and bless the seed of your seed. My origins are not yours. I was crushed by your majesty, sworn brother, crushed by your birth. Do not forget my words. Remember them at night and in the morning. Remind each other of my words. And now, kill me, quickly.'

When he had finished speaking, Chinggis answered him.

'My sworn brother set himself apart,' he said, 'and testified against us in mouthfuls. Yet I never heard that he had designs on my life. He is a man I could learn from, yet he will not become my companion. If I say "Let him die", it hardly comes into the reckoning: if I harm him without good reason, it will hardly be to my credit. He is a man of principle — and yet there is some justification for what I shall do. Tell him this. Say: "In former times Choji-darmala and Taichar stole each other's herds of horses. As a result you stirred up rebellion and advanced. At Dalan-baljut we fought, and you forced me to hide in the Jerene pass. There you frightened me. Now, when I ask you to be my companion, you refuse. I spare your life but you do not want it." Say that to Jamuqa, and say: "In answer to your words, I shall do as you bid me — I shall kill you and yet not shed your blood." '

Then he issued a decree that Jamuqa should be put to death without his blood being shed, and that his bones should not be left in the open, but should be decently buried.

It was done. Jamuqa was executed and his bones were buried.

Then in 1206, the Year of the Tiger, after Chinggis had unified the people of the felt-walled tents, they assembled at the source of the Onon river. There they hoisted the white banner with nine pennants and gave Chinggis the title 'Khan'. To Muqali they gave the title 'Guy Ong', meaning Prince, and Jebe they sent into battle, giving him orders to pursue Guchu-luk Khan of the Naiman. And having finally imposed order on the Mongolian tribes, Chinggis Khan issued a decree:

'I wish to bestow favours on all those who have served me in establishing this nation. I shall make you all commanders of units of a thousand men.'

So he decreed, naming ninety-five trusted companions to command ninety-five thousand men.

Then he issued a further decree:

'I have appointed ninety-five men — including my sons-in-law — to be commanders over ninety-five thousand. Yet there are those whom I would favour still further.' And he said: 'Let Bo'orchu, Muqali and the other commanders come forward!'

Shigi-qutuqu was with him in his yurt at the time, and Chinggis said to him: 'Go and summon them!'

But Shigi-qutuqu replied: 'What greater services have Bo'or-chu, Muqali and the others performed, and compared with whom? If there are any favours to be granted, surely I was not lacking in my service to you? I have served you fully

> from the cradle
> where I lay at your noble threshold
> till my beard sprouted
> and I became a man.
> I thought of no one else
> from the time of incontinence
> at your golden threshold
> till my beard sprouted round my mouth.
> I grew. I made no false moves.
> Mother Ho'elun made me lie at her feet,
> she raised me as her son.
> She made me lie at her side,
> she raised me as your younger brother.

Now, what favours will you grant me?'

To these words Chinggis Khan replied: 'Are you not my sixth younger brother? To you, the last-born, shall go your share of what I give to all my younger brothers. In recognition of your services, moreover, I shall allow you to commit up to nine crimes without fear of punishment.'

That was his decree. And he added: 'At the time when I, protected by Eternal Heaven, was setting the entire nation in order, you were my eyes and ears. The entire nation shall be divided between my mother, my brothers, my sons and myself. The people of the felt-walled tents shall be divided and the people of the wooden-doored dwellings shall be separated according to their tribes. And let no one presume to counter-mand your orders!'

So he decreed, and again he said:

'You must punish the thieves
and make good the lies
of the entire nation.
Kill those who should be killed.
Punish those who should be punished.'

So Shigi-qutuqu was appointed to see justice done.

Chinggis Khan also said: 'Make a register of the division of the nation, and write the shares down in a blue book, together with the judgements you have made. To the seed of my seed and beyond let no one alter Shigi-qutuqu's register, that blue writing on white paper in a blue book. Anyone who tries shall be found guilty!'

So he decreed.

But Shigi-qutuqu said: 'How can a last-born brother take the same share as all the others? If the khan favours me, let him give me my own settlement — let that be his favour!'

In these words he petitioned his khan, to which Chinggis replied: 'You have decided upon your own reward. So be it!'

Then Shigi-qutuqu, having received his favour, went out and summoned Bo'orchu, Muqali and the other commanders, and showed them into the yurt.

First Chinggis Khan addressed Father Monglik:

'You were born with me,
and we were born together.
You grew up with me
and we grew up together.
You were lucky and blessed.

You have served and protected me — how many times? I remember when the Ong Khan my father and Senggum my sworn brother tricked me and summoned me to the betrothal feast. I came, and spent the night on the way in your yurt. If you had not dissuaded me, Father Monglik, I would have gone on

into waters that whirled
and fire that flamed.

For that service alone you would be remembered by the seed

of my seed, and in memory of it you shall sit on this seat at the corner, and yearly and monthly, at the giving of gifts,* I shall show you my favour even to the seed of your seed!'

So he spoke and decreed.

Then he spoke to Bo'orchu:

'When I was small I was robbed of eight light bay geldings. I went after them for three days and three nights, and on the way I met you. You said: "You have come to me in need of help. I shall help you and be your friend and companion." You were milking your mare at the time — yet you left without a word to your father, hiding your leather bag and bucket in the field. You took my bald-tailed chestnut, and gave me your black-headed grey. Leaving your horses without a master, you mounted your swift dun and became my companion of the steppe. For three nights we pursued the thieves until, at the edge of a circular camp, we saw my stolen geldings. We stole them back there and then, escaping and driving them before us. Your father was a rich man, and you were his only son — what did you know about me when you gave me your friend-ship, when you pledged me your brave heart? I could not forget you after that. I sent Belgutei to you, saying: "Let us be friends again," and, riding a chestnut horse with a hunched back, your grey woollen cloak tied across the saddle, you came.

'When the Three Merkit attacked and circled us three times round Mount Burqan, you circled with me. And again, when I slept after the battle with the Tatar people at Dalan-nemur-ges, and the rain poured ceaselessly down, day and night, you shielded me with your cloak to keep me dry and warm. There you stood, shifting your weight from one foot to the other only once, until the night was over. Such was your courage. Is there no end to your brave acts?

'Now, Bo'orchu and Muqali, you are the ones who put me on my throne, who encouraged me in the right path and dissuaded me from doing wrong. Now I put you above all others, on the highest seats, and for up to nine crimes you

---

* This refers to the khan's practice of giving gold, silver and silks to queens and princesses to celebrate the birth of sons.

shall not be punished. Bo'orchu, your command shall be ten thousand men on the right flank, extending up the Altai.'

And of Muqali he said: 'When we pitched our camp in Qutula Khan's dancing place, in the Qorqonaq forest by the Many-Leaved Tree, I pledged my word to Muqali, in memory of his father and in honour of the omen given to him in a sign from Heaven. Now I sit upon the upper seat, and to the seed of his seed Muqali shall become prince of the entire nation!'

He conferred the title of Guy Ong on Muqali there and then, and issued a decree saying: 'Let Muqali take charge of ten thousand men on the left flank, extending up to Qara'un-jidun.'

Chinggis Khan now turned to Qorchi: 'Once you prophesied on my behalf; and for many years, since I was small until this moment,

> when it was wet, we bore the rain together,
> when it was cold, we bore the cold together.

You have always used your strength to bless me with, and at the time of your prophecy you said: "Should my prophecy come true and Heaven fulfil your desires, let me have thirty women for myself." You prophesied truly, and now I shall favour you. Feast your eyes on the fine women and girls of those subjugated peoples, and take your pick!'

So he decreed, and again: 'In addition to your command of three thousand Ba'arin soldiers, I give you command of a full unit of ten thousand men. With Taqai and Ashiq, you will take the Chinos, the To'olos and the Telenggut, and you, Qorchi, shall be in charge over all. You will pitch your camps freely along the Erdish river, as far as the people of the forest, and you will subdue those people. Let Qorchi take command of ten thousand men!'

So he decreed, saying: 'The people of the forest shall do nothing without consulting Qorchi. If they disobey, why hesitate? Punish them!'

Then Chinggis Khan addressed Jurchedei:

'You did your major service when we were fighting the

Kereyit at Qalaqaljit sands — a worrying time for us. Sworn brother Quyildar promised to protect me, but you, Jurchedei, carried out the task. You attacked the Jirgin, the Tubegen and the Dongqayid; all the important warriors were crushed by you, including Quri-shilemun with his thousand sentries. When you reached the main army you shot Senggum in the cheek with an arrow, and as a result the door was opened to me by the Almighty Spirits. If Senggum had not been wounded, what would have happened to us? That was Jurchedei's great and loyal service! Afterwards we parted from him, going downstream along the Qalqa river, but I thought of him constantly, comparing him to the shelter of a high mountain. At Lake Baljuna we stopped to water the animals. Then we rode out, and Jurchedei went ahead to scout the land. We went into battle against the Kereyit with our strength increased ten times by Heaven and Earth: we overcame and plundered them. Thus the most important tribe was razed to the ground, and the Naiman and Merkit peoples could no longer look us in the face — they turned their backs on us and scattered.

'But because of his daughters Jaqa-gambu of the Kereyit was allowed to stay with his subjects, his tribe was left intact. When he rebelled for a second time, Jurchedei played tricks to lure away those who had followed him. He siezed Jaqa-gambu and suffocated him. Then for a second time we destroyed and scattered Jaqa-gambu's people. That was Jurchedei's second service!'

> In the days of slaying and being slain
> he ignored his own safety,
> and because of this
> in the days of killing and being killed
> he fought in the front line,
> and because of this

Chinggis Khan favoured him and gave him Ibaqa-beki as a wife, saying to Ibaqa: 'It is not that you are unintelligent, or that your looks and complexion are at fault. You have been

in my heart and at my feet, and I have visited you regularly.*
Mindful of the great principle by which great deeds are
rewarded, I will favour Jurchedei, because

> in the days of fighting and being fought
> he was our shield,
> against the enemy
> he was our shelter.
> He brought together
> the scattered people,
> the divided people,
> and united them.

Mindful of that principle, I give you to him, and from now
on my seed that sits upon this throne shall know how to
reward such service. They shall not countermand my orders.
Furthermore, even to the seed of my seed Ibaqa shall never
be displaced.'

All this he spoke and decreed, saying again to Ibaqa: 'Your
father gave you two hundred servants as a dowry; he also
gave you Ashiq-temur, the Iron Helmet, and Alchiq, the Spy,
as cooks. Now that you are going to join the Uru'ut people
let me have Ashiq and a hundred of your servants as a legacy.
Now go!'

When he had taken his share of her dowry, Chinggis spoke
to Jurchedei. 'I am giving my Ibaqa to you,' he said. 'Will you
not also take charge of your four thousand Uru'ut people?'

So he decreed, bestowing his favour on Jurchedei.

---

* In those days second wives slept at their husbands' feet, while
their first wives slept beside them.

CHAPTER NINE
Chinggis Khan's military and civil administration.

THEN CHINGGIS KHAN TURNED TO QUBILAI.
'For me,' he said, 'you pressed down

> the necks of the powerful,
> the buttocks of wrestlers.

You, Qubilai, Jelme, Jebe and Sube'etei — my four hounds —
when I pointed you in the direction I wanted you to go,

> when I said "Get there!"
> you smashed through solid ores;
> when I said "Attack!"
> you split the rocks asunder.
> You broke the shining stones in pieces,
> you parted the deep waters.

I sent my four hounds like arrows to the appointed place, while my four best geldings* fought alongside me in the battle. With Jurchedei and Quyildar in the vanguard with their troops, my heart was completely at ease.'

And to show his favour he asked Qubilai: 'Will you take charge of the army's affairs? Because of Bedu'un's obstinacy I refused him his thousand men. I behaved badly to him, but he respects you and with you in charge I think he could take command. That way it could work.' And he added: 'Later we will assess his behaviour.'

Then Chinggis Khan spoke of Geniges Qunan, saying: 'For you, Bo'orchu, Muqali and the rest, this Qunan became a wolf in the night and a crow in the bright day. When we were on the move he never stopped to rest, and when we stopped to rest he stayed with us.

---

* Chinggis Khan's four generals were known as his 'four hounds', his marshals as the 'four best geldings' (see Appendix A).

With foreigners
he never adopted another face.
With my enemies
he never adopted another face.

Never act before consulting Qunan and Koko-chos. Consult them first, then act!'

So he decreed. And he added: 'Jochi is my eldest son. Qunan shall command ten thousand Geniges troops under his leadership.'

He went on: 'Qunan, Koko-chos, Degei and Old Man Usun — these four never hid what they saw from me, or concealed what they heard.'

Then Chinggis Khan turned to Jelme:

'When I was born at Deli'un-boldaq on the Onon river, Old Man Jarchi'udai came down from the Burqan-galdun carrying his bellows on his back and Jelme in his cradle. He came to give me swaddling clothes of sable. Since Jelme became my companion he has been

the slave of my threshold,
the personal slave of my door.

His services have been many;

as he was born with me, we were born together,
as he grew up with me, we grew together.

Our friendship was rooted in those sable swaddling clothes; he is fortunate and blessed in that. Even if he commits up to nine crimes, he shall not be found guilty.'

So he decreed.

Then Chinggis Khan said to Tolun: 'How can you and your father both command a separate thousand? When you were gathering the people together you were your father's right-hand man. You struggled to unite them, and because of this I gave you the title of Cherbi. Will you now, you and Turuqan together, take those you have gathered and form a single unit of a thousand men?'

So he decreed.

And again he said to Onggur the cook: 'You, Onggur, son

of Monggetu-kiyan, came with your Changshi'ut and Baya'ut kinsmen, with the Three Toqura'ut and the Five Tarqut, to form one camp for me.

> In the fog you did not go astray,
> nor did you forsake me in the battle.
> When it was wet, we bore the rain together;
> when it was cold, we bore the cold together.

Now, what kind of favour will you ask of me?'

And Onggur replied: 'If I may choose my favour, let it be this: my Baya'ut kinsmen are scattered among the tribes. Let me bring them together again.'

Then Chinggis answered: 'Let it be done. Collect your kinsmen and form a unit of a thousand men under your command.'

Again, he said: 'Onggur and Boro'ul, your job shall be to provide food for both the left flank and the right. On the right let no man, standing or sitting, go without, and on the left let no man, whether in the ranks or not, go without. If you can take charge of the provisioning, my throat will never choke and my heart will be easy. Now, both of you, ride off and distribute food to all our people.' And he added: 'When you arrange the seats to the right and left of the great kumiss flasks, you should attend to the food as well.' He pointed out their seats to them. 'There — sit with Tolun and the others, facing me, in the centre of the yurt.'

Then Chinggis Khan spoke to Boro'ul:

'You four — Shigi-qutuqu, Boro'ul, Guchu and Kokochu — came from other tribes. My mother

> found you on the ground
> and took you on her lap;
> she made you her sons,
> cared for you
> and brought you up.
> She pulled you up by the neck
> and made you the equals of all men.
> She pulled you up by the collar
> and made you the equals of all men.

She brought you up to be our shadows, the companions of her own sons. Who can count the services and benefits you have rendered since then in return for my mother's service to you? Boro'ul, you became my companion:

> on our swift expeditions on rainy nights
> you never let me pass the night
> on an empty stomach.
> When we were engaged in battle with our foes,
> you never let me pass the night
> without a stew.

When we rode against the Tatars, that vengeful people who had destroyed our fathers and our forefathers, we had our revenge: we measured them against the lynchpin and killed them off. But Qargil-shira escaped the slaughter; he got away and became a bandit. Suffering and hungry, he turned up at my mother's tent to beg.

' "I am a seeker of alms," said he.

' "If you seek alms," he was told, "you must sit over there."

'And while he was sitting on the end of the bed next to the fire by the door, Tolui, who was only five, came in from the outside. Almost immediately he ran out again, and, as he passed, Qargil-shira snatched him up, tucked him under his arm, and ran off with him, pulling a knife as he went.

'Boro'ul's wife Altani had been sitting on the other side of the tent, and, hearing my mother shout: "The boy will be killed!" she ran after Qargil-shira, seized his plaits of hair with one hand, and grasped the fist that was clutching the knife with the other. As she pulled at him, he dropped the knife.

'Meanwhile Jetei and Jelme were killing a short-horned black ox by ripping the main artery from an incision in its back. They heard Altani's cry and came running, wielding their axes, their fists red with blood. They killed Qargil-shira on the spot, and immediately everyone began to argue about which of them had saved the boy's life.

'Jelme and Jetei said: "If we had not come running when we did and killed the Tatar, he would have harmed the boy. Surely the highest merit goes to us."

'But Altani said: "If you had not heard me shouting, you'd

never have known. I ran and caught up with him, seized his plaits and grabbed his hand as he tried to draw his knife. If he had not dropped the knife he would surely have harmed the boy."

'Then everyone agreed that Altani had earned the highest merit, and in reward for her service in saving the boy's life she became like a second shaft to her husband, Boro'ul.

'And remember, Boro'ul, when we fought the Kereyit on the Qalqaljit sands, when Ogodei was hit in the neck by an arrow and fell? It was you who dismounted and stayed with him, sucking the congealed blood from his wound with your own mouth. All night you guarded him, and in the morning you put him on a horse. But Ogodei was unable to ride — so you took him on your horse, in front of you, clasping him from behind and sucking the blood from his neck until the corners of your mouth were red. You saved his life.

'Because my mother brought you up, you have served me, saving the life of my two sons,

> always alert for my summons,
> even when the call was not direct.

If Boro'ul commits up to nine crimes he shall not be punished!'

So he decreed, and he added: 'As a mark of our favour, we shall give him our daughters, and to his descendants our daughters' daughters.'

Then Chinggis Khan addressed Old Man Usun:

'Usun, Qunan, Koko-chos and Degei — these four — never hid or concealed anything they saw or heard from me. They told me everything. I had the benefit of their understanding and their thoughts. According to Mongol custom I must make one of you a *beki*. Old Man Usun is descended from the elder brother Ba'arun, so, as befits a man of his seniority, I shall make him a *beki* according to the custom.

'When he is elevated in rank

> he shall wear white robes,
> and ride a white gelding,

he shall sit on the upper seat
and there he shall be served.

Further, he shall receive gifts yearly and monthly, and shall
live in peace.'

So he decreed.

Then Chinggis Khan said: 'Because my sworn brother
Quyildar gave his life for me in battle before anyone else
had opened his mouth, his children shall receive an orphan's
recompense from generation to generation.'

So he decreed.

And to Chaqan-qo'a's son, Narin-to'oril, he said: 'Your
father fought bravely for my sake at Dalan-baljut, and was
killed there by Jamuqa. Now let To'oril take an orphan's
recompense for his father's service!'

When he heard this To'oril answered: 'If you would favour
me, grant me this: my Negus kinsmen are scattered among
other tribes. I would like to bring them together again.'

Then Chinggis Khan issued a decree: 'If you so wish, collect
your kinsmen together, and take charge of them yourself, to
the seed of your seed.'

So he decreed.

Then Chinggis Khan said to Sorqan-shira:

'When I was small, Tarqutai-kiriltuq of the Tayyichi'ut and
his kinsmen envied me. They took me prisoner, but you,
Sorqan-shira, saw through their envy. With your sons and
daughters you cared for me, hid me and released me from
captivity. I have remembered that service of yours in my
dreams through many black nights and kept it in my breast
through many bright days. I thought continuously of you,
though you took your time to come to me. If I now want
to favour you, what kind of favour would you like from
me?'

And Sorqan-shira, with his two sons, Chila'un and Chimbai, said: 'If you would favour us, grant us the Merkit land
along the Selengge river for our camps. Any further favours
I leave to my khan to decide.'

At that Chinggis Khan said: 'Let the Merkit lands be yours
to pitch your camps on. Furthermore, to the seed of your seed

you shall carry quivers. You shall be free men and shall drink the ceremonial wine. For up to nine crimes you shall not be found guilty.'

So he decreed, and he extended his favour further to Chi-la'un and Chimbai, saying:

'I remember the words you both spoke to me and would like to know how I can reward you. Whatever is in your mind, speak out. If you lack for anything, ask for it. Don't let me discover your desires through someone else — tell me yourselves, in person, with your own mouths, what you are thinking and what you lack.'

So he decreed.

Again he said: 'Sorqan-shira, Badai and Kishliq, you are freedmen. When next you gallop after our enemies you may keep whatever plunder you find; when you hunt the wild beasts you may keep whatever you kill.'

So he decreed, adding: 'Speaking of Sorqan-shira, we are reminded that he was no more than a servant to the Tayyichi'ut. As for Badai and Kishiliq, they were merely Yeke-cheren's herdsmen. Yet I have raised them to be quiver-bearers, to drink the ceremonial wine, and to enjoy all the fruits of freedom.'

Then Chinggis Khan addressed Naya'a.

'Once,' he said, 'Old Man Shirgotu seized Tarqutai-kiriltuq with the help of his two sons, and planned to bring him to me. You, Naya'a, were one of those sons, and on the way you said to your father: "How can we go on with this — capturing our rightful khan and forsaking him?" Instead you released him and came to me with your story. You, nicknamed "the Lark", spoke up and said: "We laid hands on our rightful khan and thought to bring him to you. But we found we could not forsake him, so we let him go. We have come to serve Chinggis Khan. Had we come to him after forsaking our own khan he would never have trusted us. We could not forsake him." I approved of Naya'a's words, because he remembered one of the great principles — that of loyalty. That was why he could not forsake his khan. I said to myself: "I shall rely on this man for one task." Now, having given Bo'orchu command of the ten thousand men on the right, and Muqali command

of the ten thousand men on the left, I give Naya'a command
of the ten thousand men in the centre.'

So he decreed.

And he said: 'Let Jebe and Sube'etei form units one thousand strong from the men they have gathered together.'

And he asked Degei the Shepherd to select a further thousand from those who were still without a leader.

Then he turned to Guchugur the Carpenter: 'You lack men,'
he said. 'Mulqalqu of the Jadaran has been, like you, my
constant companion. Why don't the two of you put together
a unit of a thousand men between you?'

All those who had helped Chinggis Khan to establish the
nation and had toiled with him to make it secure were made
commanders of a thousand men. All those who deserved
favour were favoured, and all those who deserved praise were
praised. Within the units of a thousand men he appointed
commanders over groups of a hundred, and within those
over groups of ten. The main units he made part of larger
contingents of ten thousand, appointing commanders to rule
over them. He granted them his favour in a decree, saying: 'I
have shown favour to the commanders of ten thousand men
and one thousand men according to their merits.'

Then he issued a further decree:

'Formerly I had eighty night-guards and seventy sentries
standing guard in shifts. Now, by Eternal Heaven and by
Heaven and Earth, my might has been so increased that the
whole nation has been united under my rule. Choose therefore
sentries from within the units of a thousand men and enter
them in my service. Take more night-guards and quiver-
bearers into my service too, to a total of ten thousand men.'

Then Chinggis Khan issued a proclamation concerning the
choosing of guards and their entry into his service:

'Let the sons of the commanders of one thousand men and
of a hundred men enter my service as guards. And let the sons
of ordinary people — those who are skilful, strong, handsome
and fit to serve at our side — also enter our service. The sons
of the commanders of a thousand men shall bring ten companions with them, and each companion shall bring a younger
brother to take his place if necessary. The sons of the com-

manders of a hundred men shall bring five companions each, and they too shall bring younger brothers to back them up. As for the sons of the commanders of ten men and the sons of ordinary people, they shall bring three companions, each with a younger brother. Let them all be released from their units, together with their horses, to strengthen the army which will serve at my side. Their chosen companions shall also be released from their original units and given to their new leaders. Apart from what they already own or have inherited, and apart from any men or geldings they have acquired on their own account, let everything be levied at a rate which we shall fix, and, once agreed, let it be carried out. In the same way, apart from their personal share, let the sons of the commanders of a hundred men be given a levy of five companions, while the sons of the commanders of ten, and those of ordinary men, be allowed three.'

So he decreed.

And again he said: 'As soon as my decree reaches the commanders of the thousands, hundreds and tens of men, and has been heard by the people in general, let it be obeyed. If anyone transgresses, he shall be found guilty and punished. If anyone who enters my service evades his shift, finds his duties too onerous, or is simply not willing to serve at my side, let him be gone, and let another man have his place. Punish those who transgress and exile them out of my sight.'

And he added: 'Do not discourage those who are willing to serve us and who want to learn by being at our side.'

Then the night-guards gathered according to Chinggis Khan's decree. Where there had been eighty before, there were now eight hundred, and Chinggis said: 'Add more to bring the contingent up to a full thousand.' Then he repeated: 'Never discourage anyone from entering my service as a night-guard.' And he appointed Yeke-ne'urin to command his night-guard of a thousand men.

Formerly he had chosen four hundred quiver-bearers. 'Let Jelme's son, Yisun-te'e, command the quiver-bearers,' he declared, 'and let him consult with Tuge's son, Bugidei. The quiver-bearers shall serve with the sentries, shift by shift. Yisun-te'e shall head one shift, Bugidei another, Horqudaq the third and Lablaqa the fourth. They shall serve and carry their quivers during each shift and shall take charge of them. Yisun-te'e will expand the unit to a full thousand men, and shall be in overall command.'

Increasing the unit of sentries who had formerly entered into his service under Ogele-cherbi to a thousand men, Chinggis Khan then said: 'Let Ogele-cherbi take overall command.'

Then he divided up the rest into units of a thousand each under the command of Dodai-cherbi, Dolqolqu-cherbi, Chanai and Aqutai. To Arqai-qasar he gave command of a thousand sentries who were also his chosen warriors. 'In days of peace let them be sentries,' he decreed, 'but in time of war they shall fight before me as warriors.'

So he decreed.

He chose a total of eight thousand men to become sentries, and two further units of a thousand each to be night-guards and quiver-bearers. Then he issued a further decree, saying:

'Once we have trained and strengthened the ten thousand guards who are closest to us, let them become the core of the army.'

Then Chinggis Khan said:

'Now I shall appoint elders to head each shift. Buqa, Alchidai, Dodai-cherbi and Dolqolqu-cherbi shall set their guards in order and send them in to me.' And he issued a proclamation, saying: 'At the beginning of each shift, the appointed commander shall be at his post to hold a roll call. Each shift shall last three nights before it is relieved by another shift. Should any guard abandon his post, his commander shall teach him a lesson with three strokes of the rod. If the same man abandons his post for a second time, he shall be punished with seven strokes of the rod. And if he abandons his post for the third time, without the permission of his commander or the excuse of physical illness, but simply because it is too much for him, let him be punished with thirty-seven strokes of the rod and then exiled to a distant place.'

So he decreed, and he added: 'The elders of the guard shall proclaim this decree at every third shift. If they fail they shall be found guilty, and if, in spite of my decree, any man transgresses it and interrupts the shift, he shall also be found guilty.'

So he decreed.

And he said: 'Elders of the guard, let none of you take it upon yourselves to reprimand any guard who has entered my service on an equal footing, just because you are now his senior. If any man offends against my law, report him to me! If anyone is to be executed, I shall be his executioner. If anyone is to be beaten, I shall make him lie down and shall beat him myself. If any one of you makes a move towards those of my guards who were once your equal, to punish them with hands or feet or with the rod, merely because you are now their seniors, you shall be repaid in kind. If you beat them with a rod, you shall be beaten with a rod in return; if with fists, then with fists you too shall be beaten.'

Once more Chinggis Khan issued a decree:

'My guards shall outrank the leaders of all the other units of a thousand, and my guards' attendants shall outrank the leaders of all other units of a hundred and of ten. If any man from an outside unit tries to set himself up against one of my guards as an equal in a dispute, then his leader shall be punished for it!'

So he decreed. And again he issued a proclamation to the commanders of the shifts:

'The quiver-bearers and sentries shall perform their day's duties, each following their chosen path. At sunset they shall give way to the guards and shall go outside to spend the night. The guards shall spend the night with us. The quiver-bearers shall leave their quivers with the night-guards before they go, and the cooks their bowls and cooking vessels. They will all spend the night outside in the place where the horses are tethered, and will remain there until we have eaten our morning stew. Once we have finished, they will report to the night-guard and their quivers and cooking pots will be restored to them, along with their rightful positions. Every shift shall follow the same rules.'

So he decreed.

And he said: 'If any man crosses in front or behind my

palace-yurt after sunset, seize him. The night-guard shall watch him all night and he will be questioned on the following morning. When the shifts are changed, those coming in should hand over their badges of office, and those going off-duty should do likewise. During the night the guards shall lie down around the palace-yurt, keeping close to the door. Those guards who remain on their feet shall smash the skulls of anyone who tries to enter, hacking at their shoulders until they fall and casting them aside. If anyone comes with an urgent message, he must tell the night-guard, and then, surrounded by guards, must report his message from the back of the yurt.

'No one shall sit behind the sentry-post,' he said, 'and no one shall enter without permission. No one shall walk behind the guard and our troops shall seize any man who tries to walk between them. If any man asks a night-guard for his number, the guard shall arrest him and seize the gelding he rode that day, his saddle, his bridle, and even the clothes he stands up in.'

So he decreed — and this was how Eljigedei, even though he was trusted, came to be captured by the night-guard when he came up behind them.

CHAPTER TEN

The empire expands.
The defiance of Teb-tenggeri.

THIS HYMN WAS RECITED BY CHINGGIS KHAN
to those who guarded him:

> 'My elder night-guards,
> who, in the cloudy night,
> lie about my tent
> with its smoke-hole,
> they have secured
> my sound and peaceful sleep
> and raised me to my throne.
> My blessed night-guards,
> who, in the starry night,
> lie about my palace,
> they have secured
> a bed for me, free of fear,
> and raised me to my high throne.
> My night-guards, loyal and true,
> sleepless they stand
> in the blustering snowstorms,
> in shivering cold,
> around my latticed yurt.
> They eased my heart
> and raised me to my happy throne.
> My guards, the trusted ones,
> standing around my felt-skirted tent
> in the midst of the simmering foe,
> have watched over me
> without blinking an eye.
> My guards, the strenuous ones,
> were quick to defend me
> when the birch-bark quivers rattled.
> My guards, so swift to action,
> were quick to defend me

when the willow-wood quivers rattled.
Thus I call them blessed
and name them "Elder Night-Guards".

Let the seventy sentries who came into my service with Ogole-
cherbi also be renamed — they shall be called my "Noble
Sentries". And let Arqai's warriors be called the "Elder Warriors".

The quiver-bearers,
Bugidei and Yisun-te'e,
"Noble Quiver-Bearers"
from now on shall be.'

So he decreed.

Then Chinggis Khan said: 'As for my ten thousand personal
guards, specially chosen from the ranks of nineteen thousand
men to be my bodyguard, they will be my legacy to my sons
who shall sit after me on my throne. Care for them well and
ensure their contentment. Have I not decreed that they shall
be called my strong and blessed ones?'

And he added: 'The night-guards shall take charge of the
houseboys, the camel-herders, the cow-herders and the atten-
dant girls of the palace. They shall also look after the palace-
yurt carts, the banners, drums, pikes and spears, as well as
the cooking vessels. They shall be responsible for our food
and drink, and shall direct the cooking of the uncut meat.
If we lack food or meat we shall look to the night-guards
to supply it. The quiver-bearers will undertake the distrib-
ution, but only with the night-guards' permission, and
they shall serve the night-guards first.' And he said: 'The
night-guards shall control all those entering or leaving the
palace-yurt. Two shall act as door-keepers at the tent door,
while two more shall bring in the great kumiss flasks.' And
he said: 'They shall appoint camp masters to go ahead and
set up the palace-tent. When we go hunting or flying our
falcons together, half the night-guards will accompany us,
while the other half remains at the camp, looking after the
carts.'

Then Chinggis Khan added: 'The night-guards shall never go to war, unless we ourselves decide to fight.' And he added another command: 'Any commander who, jealous of the night-guards, sends them out to war without my permission, will be found guilty and punished. You may ask why I don't want my guards to be sent to war like other soldiers. The answer is that they are here to guard my golden life, and that alone. They will accompany me in my hunting and my falconry and endure what I endure. As administrators of my palace, whether at rest or on the move, they will also look after the waggons. Do you imagine it is easy to guard my person? Do you think it is easy to look after the great carts, whether at rest or on the move? The night-guards, I repeat, have more than their fair share of duties, and their responsibilities are many and various. Therefore I say that they should not go to war except at my command.'

Again he issued a decree saying: 'Some of my night-guards will take charge of judicial matters. They will listen to cases, and, with Shigi-qutuqu, pass judgement. Some will look after the quivers, bows, armour and equipment, ready to distribute them when they are needed. They will take some of the geldings, load up the hunting nets and be ready to move. Some of the guards, together with the stewards, will take charge of distributing the general effects.'

And he said: 'When the guards have assigned the quiver-bearers and the sentries to their camps, the quiver-bearers belonging to Yisun-te'e and Bugidei shall serve on the right hand of the palace with the sentries belonging to Alchidai, Ogole and Aqutai. Buqa, Dodai-cherbi, Dolqolqu-cherbi, Chanai and the other sentries shall serve on my left, and Arqai's brave warriors shall do duty in front of the palace.'

And he said: 'After they have dealt with the palace waggons, the night-guards shall serve next to the palace on the left and the right. Dodai-cherbi will remain in the palace and assess the guards constantly — all the sentries who are on duty at any given moment, together with the houseboys, the horse-herders, the shepherds, the camel-herders and cattle-herders.'

These were the appointments made by Chinggis Khan, and

he proclaimed: 'Let Dodai-cherbi always be there, serving at
the rear of the palace,

> eating left-over scraps,
> warming himself with cakes and dried horse-
> dung.'*

Chinggis Khan sent Qubilai-noyan out to do battle with
the Qarlu'ut; but before they had a chance to fight, the Arslan
Khan submitted to Qubilai. He was immediately brought
before Chinggis Khan for an audience. Because he had not
put up any resistance, Chinggis Khan favoured his cause and
issued a decree, saying: 'We shall give him our daughter in
marriage.'

Meanwhile Sube'etei-ba'atur had pursued the sons of Toqto'a of the Merkit in a cart reinforced with iron. He caught
up with them at the Chui river, slaughtered them all, and returned to camp.

Jebe, meanwhile, had gone after Guchuluk Khan of the
Naiman. Catching up with him at the Yellow cliff, he finished
him off and returned to camp.

The Idu'ut of the Ui'ud then sent emissaries to Chinggis
Khan, bearing this petition:

> 'Like the clouds parting
> to reveal our mother sun,
> like the ice cracking
> to reveal the river water,

so the name and fame of Chinggis Khan have been revealed
to me, and I rejoice in it. If the khan would favour me, if he
would give me

> a link of his golden belt,
> a thread from his scarlet garment,

then I would become his fifth son, and would serve him.'

This was his petition, and Chinggis Khan approved of it,

---

* Horse-dung was an inferior fuel: the implication is that Dodai will
be too busy to look after himself properly — his appointment was
an honour none the less.

Chinggis Khan at the gates of Jungdu: 'He went on to surround
Jungdu, laying siege to it, and sending his soldiers to do
the same to other neighbouring towns and cities' (*page 134*)

'During that campaign Chinggis Khan made the Altan Khan submit,
and exacted satin from him in large quantities' (*page 137*)

saying: 'He shall become my fifth son and I shall give him my daughter in marriage. Invite him to come to us bringing gold and silver, pearls both large and small, damasks and silks.'

That was his message and the Idu'ut rejoiced because he had found favour. Bringing gold and silver, silks, brocades, damasks and satins, and pearls both large and small, he presented himself for an audience with Chinggis Khan. There Chinggis Khan bestowed his favour upon him and gave him his daughter, Al-altun, in marriage.

In 1207, the Year of the Hare, Chinggis Khan commanded Jochi to ride out with the soldiers of the right flank against the people of the forest. Buqa went as guide. First Quduqa-beki of the Oyirat came ahead of his tribe of ten thousand to submit. He met Jochi and guided him to where his tribe was camped at Shiqshit. There they all submitted to him. After that the Oyirat, Buriyat, Bargun, Ursut, Qabqanas Kangqas and Tubas tribes also submitted to Jochi, along with ten thousand Kirgisut soldiers and their lords. They came to Jochi bringing white gerfalcons, white geldings and black sables, to seek audience with him and join his army.

So Jochi began to subjugate the forest peoples. The Shibir, Kesdiyim, Bayit, Tuqas, Tenlek, To'eles, Tas and Bajigid tribes came over to our side. Then Jochi sent for the Kirgisut leaders of ten thousand men and the leaders of a thousand, and brought them back for an audience with Chinggis Khan. They came, presenting him with the white gerfalcons, white geldings and black sables. Chinggis Khan received Quduqa-beki of the Oyirat with special favour because he had sub-mitted before the others, and had led his ten thousand men to join our army.

Then Chinggis Khan gave Checheyigen as a wife to his son Inalchi, while to Inalchi's elder brother, Torolchi, he gave Jochi's daughter, Qoluyiqan, which means 'goddess'. Alaqa-beki he gave to the ruler of the Onggut, and he showed favour to Jochi, saying:

'You, the eldest of my sons, have made your first foray from my tent. Your journey has been a smooth one—you lost neither men nor geldings, and you subjugated the fortunate peoples of the forest without bloodshed. You came back safely: therefore all these people shall be yours.'

So he decreed.

Boro'ul-noyan was sent out meanwhile to fight against the Qori-tumet. When the lord of that tribe had died, his place had been taken by his wife, Botoqui-tarqun, which means the Fat Fierce One. Approaching Tumet territory, Boro'ul went ahead of the main force with a three-man party, and in the late evening, as they travelled along a trail in the dense forest, they were taken unawares by Tumet watchmen and ambushed. Boro'ul was captured and killed, and when Chinggis Khan heard about it he was very angry. He would have ridden out against the enemy himself, but Bo'orchu and Muqali both counselled strongly against it. Eventually Chinggis Khan gave in, and appointed instead Dorbei-doqshin of the Dorbet, saying:

'Order the soldiers in strict ranks, pray to the Almighty Spirits, and do not give in until the Tumet people submit!'

So he decreed.

The soldiers were ordered into ranks, and decoys were sent out along the roads and trails guarded by the enemy to deceive them. They even infiltrated the enemy passes in order to distract the sentries. Then Chinggis Khan ordered the real army to travel in the paths made by the deer and other animals. If any man fell by the wayside he was to be beaten, and the cooks and drivers carried ten sticks each on their backs for this purpose. All the axes, adzes, saws, chisels and other tools carried by the cooks and drivers were laid out in order, and the soldiers were instructed to chop, saw, and hack down any vegetation in their path, to clear it for the attack. In this way they ascended the mountain and came on the Tumet people so suddenly that it was as if they fell on them through the very smoke-holes of their tents. They took them by surprise as they were feasting and plundered them.

Earlier Qorchi-noyan and Quduqa-beki had been captured by the Tumet and they were there in the camp. This was what had happened to Qorchi: when Chinggis Khan had decreed that he could choose thirty wives from among the Tumet beauties, Qorchi had gone straight off to make his choice. But

although the Tumet had submitted earlier, now they decided
to fight back and they took Qorchi prisoner. When Chinggis
Khan heard this he appointed Quduqa to rescue him, thinking
that he understood the ways of the forest people. But he too
was captured. So now that the Tumet people were subjugated
once and for all, Chinggis Khan immediately gave a hundred
of them to Boro'ul's family in compensation for his death.
Qorchi got his thirty girls and Quduqa-beki received Botoqui-
tarqun as a wife.

Then Chinggis Khan issued a decree:

'I shall divide all my subject peoples between my mother,
my sons, and my younger brothers.'

And he added: 'In gathering the nation together, one of
those who endured most was my mother. Jochi is my eldest
son, and Otchigin the youngest of my brothers.'

He gave ten thousand people to his mother, including Otchigin's share. His mother resented this, thinking she deserved
more, but she kept her mouth shut. To Jochi Chinggis Khan
gave five thousand people; to Cha'adai, his second son, eight
thousand; to Ogodei, five thousand; to Tolui, five thousand;
to Qasar, four thousand; to Alchidai, two thousand, and to
Belgutei, one thousand five hundred. But of Da'ritai, his uncle,
who had joined the Kereyit, he said: 'Get him out of my sight
and make an end of him.'

Then Bo'orchi, Muqali and Shigi-qutuqu, all three of them,
spoke up:

'That would be like putting out your own fire or breaking
down your own tent,' they said. 'Your uncle is the sole
reminder of your father, the only remaining link. How can
you forsake him? Don't be too hard on him — he did not
know what he was doing. Let him stay with his family, and
let the smoke of their fires rise up from the camp of your good
father's youth.'

They went on speaking to him like this until it was as if the
smoke had got into his nose and eyes, and he wept. He
accepted their frankness and agreed with them, saying: 'You
are right. Let him be.' Thus Bo'orchu, Muqali and Shigi-
qutuqu were able to quieten his wrath.

Then Chinggis Khan said: 'I shall appoint four military

leaders to be advisers; and I give ten thousand men to my mother and Otchigan: their advisers shall be Guchu, Kokochu, Jungsai and Qorqasun. To Jochi I shall give three advisers — Qunan, Mongke'ur and Kete; and Cha'adai shall also have three — Qarachar, Mongke and Idoqudai.' And he added: 'Cha'adai is obstinate and narrow-minded. Make sure that Koko-chos stays with him morning and night to help and advise him.'

So he decreed. And he continued: 'Ogodei shall have two advisers — Iluge and Degei — and Tolui two also — Jedei and Bala. I appoint Jebke as Qasar's adviser and Char'urqai as Alchidar's.'

Father Monglik had seven sons. The middle one was called Kokochu Teb-tenggeri, and the seven of them joined forces to attack Qasar. Qasar immediately reported this to Chinggis Khan, kneeling before him and telling him that he had been beaten by the seven Qongqotan brothers. Chinggis Khan was extremely angry and interrupted his story to say:

'You used to say that no one could ever defeat you. How could you have been beaten?'

At this Qasar wept and, getting to his feet, left the yurt. He was angry with his brother and did not go near him for three days. Then Teb-tenggeri said:

'By the Almighty Spirits, Khan, do not forget that although it was once predicted that Temujin should rule the nation, it was also predicted once that Qasar should. If you do not attack him quickly Heaven knows what might happen.'

When he heard this, Chinggis Khan mounted and rode out that very night to capture Qasar. As soon as he had gone Guchu and Kokochu reported to Mother Ho'elun, and that very night she harnessed her white camel to her black-framed covered cart, and set out after him. She travelled all night, catching up with him just after sunrise. Chinggis Khan had tied Qasar's sleeves together, removed his hat and sash, and was interrogating him. He was surprised by his mother's arrival and frightened by it. She was very angry, and, dismounting from her cart, she immediately untied Qasar's sleeves and released him. She also gave him back his hat and sash.

Then, unable to contain her fury, she sat down cross-legged and exposed her breasts to them, saying: 'Look at them! These are the breasts that suckled you. These . . . ' and here she quoted all the old proverbs, going over and over them. 'Those are they who gnawed their own afterbirth and cut their own birthcords. What has Qasar done? Temujin could suck one breast dry when he was young, Qachi'un and Otchigin could not finish a breast between them. But Qasar — he could suck two full breasts until they sagged. He set my breasts free and made them comfortable. To my mind therefore my Temujin is the one with knowledge, he has skills of the mind, while my Qasar is powerful and skilled at shooting. Because of this

> he fired at those
> who shot at him,
> and forced them to submit.
> He shot long-distance arrows
> at those who fled in fear,
> and forced them to submit.

I suppose now that you have finished off all your enemies, you can't bear to look on Qasar.'

After he had calmed her down, Chinggis Khan said: 'Mother, I have made you furious:

> being afraid, I showed my fear,
> being ashamed, I showed my shame.

We will withdraw,' he said. And they withdrew.

But unknown to Mother Ho'elun, he secretly took away Qasar's men, leaving him with only one thousand four hundred people. When his mother discovered this, the thought of it killed her prematurely — it happened very quickly — and Jebke, who had been assigned to Qasar as an adviser by Chinggis Khan, grew frightened. He ran away to Barqujin.

In 1210 the peoples of the Nine Tongues* began to rally to Teb-tenggeri's banner, and there were soon many more of

---

* i.e. of many different languages.

them than were gathered in Chinggis Khan's horse-tethering place. While they were gathering, Temuge-otchigin's people went to join them and Otchigin was obliged to send Soqor as an emissary to ask for their return. Teb-tenggeri was contemptuous. 'You and Otchigin', he said, 'are nothing but women, both of you, and you think to have an ambassador?' Then he beat Soqor soundly and made him carry his saddle back to Otchigin on foot.

When Otchigin heard this, he went himself to Teb-tenggeri and said: 'When I sent my emissary you beat him and sent him back on foot. Now I have come myself to request the return of my people.'

Then the seven Qongqotan brothers closed in on him and taunted him, saying: 'You were right to send your emissary, Soqor.'

Otchigin was afraid he would be captured and beaten. 'No,' he said, 'I was wrong to send my emissary.'

'If you were wrong,' the seven brothers said, 'kneel down and plead.'

So he knelt down behind Teb-tenggeri, and they sent him home without his people.

Early next morning, while Chinggis Khan was still in bed, Otchigin came to him in tears. He knelt before his brother and said: 'The peoples of the Nine Tongues have flocked to join Teb-tenggeri, and, when I sent an emissary to him to request the return of my own subject people, he was beaten and sent back to me on foot, his saddle on his back. When I went myself, the seven brothers blocked my path this way and that, and made me kneel down and plead with Teb-tenggeri.'

He was weeping as he said it, but before Chinggis Khan could utter a word, Lady Borte sat up in bed, covering her breast with the edge of the quilt. When she saw Otchigin weeping, she wept herself and said:

'What are the Qongqotan doing? Recently they joined forces to beat Qasar, and now they make Otchigin kneel down behind them. What is going on? Our brothers are like cypresses and pines; they will be harmed and undermined by this behaviour. Later on

when your body, withered as a tree,
comes crashing down,
who will be able to govern
that tangle of hemp, your people?
When your body, like the stone base of a column,
crumbles and falls down,
who will be able to govern
that flock of red-polls,
your people?

If these people would secretly harm your younger brothers, who are like cypresses and pines, they will hardly allow three or four untried youngsters — our sons — to hold power until they are grown up. What have the Qongqotan done? They have humiliated your younger brothers. How can you sit there?' And Lady Borte wept bitterly.

Then Chinggis Khan said to Otchigin: 'Teb-tenggeri is on his way towards us now. You are in charge. Do whatever you like to him.'

At that Otchigin got to his feet, wiped his tears and went out. He forewarned three strong men and lined them up ready. Soon after, Father Monglik entered, his seven sons with him, and Teb-tenggeri sat down on the right-hand side of the kumiss flasks.

Then Otchigin seized Teb-tenggeri's collar and said: 'Yesterday you made me plead. Now let us try each other's strength.'

Holding his collar, he pulled him towards the door, but Teb-tenggeri resisted him, and, facing him, grasped his collar in return and wrestled with him there. As they wrestled, Teb-tenggeri's hat fell behind the hearth fire. Father Monglik picked it up, smelt it and tucked it into his bosom. Then Chinggis Khan said: 'Go outside and compete for the wrestling honours.'

As Otchigin went out, pulling Teb-tenggeri behind him, his three strong men were waiting on the threshold. Together they hauled him off and broke his spine, throwing his body beyond the carts on the eastern side of the yurts. Then Otchigin went back to Chinggis Khan, saying:

'Teb-tenggeri made me plead with him, but when I suggested we should wrestle with each other he refused: he made excuses and fell to the ground. He was only a fair-weather companion.'

Then Father Monglik realised what had happened, and he wept and said:

> 'Since the huge earth
> was nothing but a clod,
> since the oceans and rivers
> were no more than little streams

I have been your companion.'

And as he spoke his remaining six sons blocked the doorway and stood round the fire, rolling up their sleeves.

Chinggis Khan was wary of being crowded. 'Yield,' he said, 'and let me pass.'

As soon as he got outside, his sentries and quiver-bearers encircled him, standing round him. He saw then that Teb-tenggeri had had his spine broken and had been cast aside, so he ordered a small grey tent to be erected over his body. Then he said: 'Get the transport ready and prepare to move out.'

After they had put Teb-tenggeri's body inside the small tent, they closed the smoke-hole and wedged the door shut. A guard was set outside, but at the end of the third night, as dawn was breaking, Teb-tenggeri opened the smoke-hole and rose out of it bodily. They opened the door and realised that the slain man had indeed left the tent. Chinggis Khan said: 'Because he laid hands on my younger brothers, and spread slander among them, Heaven did not love him, and his life and his body have been spirited away.'

And he reprimanded Father Monglik: 'Because you did not curb your sons' ambition they came to think they were our equals. You were the one who risked Teb-tenggeri's head. When I realised your ambition I should have dealt with you as I did with Jamuqa, Altan, Quchar and the rest.'

But after he had finished he said: 'If I should make a promise in the morning and break it in the evening, or if I should make a promise in the evening and break it in the morning, I should be shamed and belittled. I made a promise to you once before. Let that suffice.' Then he calmed down and showed Father

Monglik his favour again. 'If only you could have reined in your overweening nature, who could have compared with your descendants?' he asked.

With the death of Teb-tenggeri, the morale of the Qong-qotan withered and died.

CHAPTER ELEVEN
The campaign against the Kitat. Chinggis Khan's last campaigns. He chooses his successor.

AFTER THAT, IN THE YEAR OF THE SHEEP, 1211, Chinggis Khan rode out against the Kitat people of northern China. He conquered Wujiu, the Black city, crossed the Pass of the Fox, and stormed the city of Sondeiwu. Jebe was then sent ahead with Guyigunek-ba'atur to scout the area, and when they reached the Chabchiyal pass, north-west of Jungdu,* they found it well guarded.

Then Jebe turned back, saying: 'We will lure them out of the pass and persuade them to follow us. Then we can turn and fight them.'

When the Kitat soldiers saw him retreating they decided to go after him. They pursued him until the valleys and mountains were choked with Kitat soldiers. Jebe lured them on until he reached a spur in the Sondeiwu mountain, then he and his men reined in their horses and turned to face the oncoming foe. They launched themselves against this ever-increasing enemy and overcame them.

Chinggis Khan was following close behind with the main body of the army. He scattered the Kitat people and defeated the brave and powerful soldiers of the Juyin and Jurchet tribes, slaughtering them until their bodies were piled up like rotten logs even to the Chabchiyal gate. Then Jebe stormed the gate itself, while Chinggis Khan attacked the passes and crossed over them, setting up his camp finally on Shira-dektur, the Yellow terrace. He went on to surround Jungdu, laying siege to it, and sending his soldiers to do the same to other neighbouring towns and cities. Jebe he sent to besiege Dungchang,† but when Jebe got there he was unable to mount

* Peking, now Beijing.
† Now Mukden, in Manchuria.

an attack so he retreated. For six days he withdrew, until the enemy was satisfied that he had gone away. Then he reined in his horsemen and turned to launch a second attack. He and his men took fresh horses and travelled through the night in order to take the enemy by surprise. The city of Dungchang fell to them immediately.

After his victory, in early 1213, Jebe came back to join Chinggis Khan. By then Jungdu had been surrounded and was under attack. But the Ongging-chingsang, the great lord over Altan Khan, petitioned him, saying:

'Heaven and Earth have decreed that the time has come for a change of dynasty. The Mongols have come down upon us in strength. They have overwhelmed our best and most powerful soldiers, and have slaughtered them all. They have captured our most impenetrable pass. If we gather our scattered forces and send them out again against the Mongols, they will take the first opportunity to slip away to their own towns. What's more, if we insist on mobilising them against their will, they will soon become our enemies, not our friends.

'Altan Khan, if you love us, submit to these Mongols, at least for the time being. Parley with them. If they withdraw we can discuss other possibilities. I've heard that this place is proving unhealthy for their men and their horses — many of them are falling sick with fever. Let's give their khan a princess and generously distribute gold and silver, satin and other goods to his soldiers. How else can we know whether or not he will accept our proposal?'

Altan Khan approved of the idea. 'If that's how you feel,' he said, 'so be it.'

He submitted to Chinggis Khan and presented him with a princess named Chi-kuo. To the soldiers he generously distributed gold and silver, satin and other goods from Jungdu city — as much as he thought they would carry. Then he sent Ongging-chingsang to submit to Chinggis Khan.

Chinggis Khan accepted the Ongging's proposal. He sent orders that the soldiers besieging the surrounding towns should withdraw, and this they did. Then Ongging-chingsang accompanied Chinggis Khan and his army as far as the Mojiu and Wijiu mountain spurs before turning back. Chinggis Khan's soldiers loaded their mounts with as much gold, silver, satin and other goods as they could carry, tying their loads on with silk. Then they departed.

During the same campaign Chinggis also advanced on the Qashin people. As soon as his army arrived, Burqan Khan,* the leader of the Qashin tribe, said: 'I submit, and shall serve you by becoming the right hand of your army.'

He presented Chinggis Khan with a princess named Chaqa. 'When we heard the name of Chinggis Khan', he said, 'and knew of his fame, we were filled with awe. Now you have arrived in person, in all your might, and we are indeed filled with awe. In awe we Tangqut people offer ourselves as your right hand, to serve you.'

And he added: 'At this time we have

> established camps
> and solid cities.

As your companions

> when you are executing
> a swift campaign,
> when you are fighting
> a sharp battle,

we shall not be able to keep up with you, to fight your swift campaign, your sharp battle, for you. But if you favour us, your Tangqut people

> will present you with many camels,
> reared in the shelter of the broom-grass
> and given as a levy.
> As weavers of woollen cloth
> and makers of satin,
> we will give them to you.
> As trainers of falcons,
> we will gather them for you.

---

* Burqan Khan means 'Buddhist ruler' and the Qashin was a Buddhist tribe.

We want you to have the best.'

So he petitioned, and he kept his word. He levied camels from the Tangqut people until it was impossible to drive any more before him, and he brought them to Chinggis Khan and gave them to him.

During that campaign Chinggis Khan made the Altan Khan submit, and exacted satin from him in large quantities. He made the Burqan Khan submit, and took many camels from him. In that Year of the Sheep, 1211, Altan Khan, whose name was Aqutai, submitted to him, as did the Iluqu-burqan of the Tangqut people. Chinggis returned in triumph and pitched his camp on the Sa'ari steppe.

Jubqan, meanwhile, had been sent out at the head of a trade delegation to seek allegiances beyond our borders. But when, in the Year of the Dog, 1214, Jubqan found his path obstructed by Aqutai, the Altan Khan of the Kitat people, Chinggis Khan decided to ride out against them.

'They've already submitted to me once,' he said. 'How can they now block my emissaries on their way to the frontier?'

So he rode out. Aiming at the Tunggon pass, Chinggis Khan sent Jebe ahead through Chabchiyal. But the Altan Khan, anticipating Chinggis's plans, called up Ile, Qada and Hobogetur and put them in charge of his best soldiers. His best fighting force, the Red Jackets, he deployed in the vanguard, saying: 'Go and defend the Tunggon pass. Whatever you do, don't let them cross the ridge.' Then he quickly ordered his three commanders and their soldiers to move forward.

As a result, when Chinggis Khan reached the pass he found so many Kitat soldiers in his path that the ground could hardly bear the weight of them. Chinggis engaged with the three commanders, forcing Ile and Qada to give ground. He brought Tolui and his son-in-law Chugu up, and sent them into the attack from the flanks, forcing the Red Jackets to retreat. As Ile and Qada withdrew, Chinggis Khan's soldiers overwhelmed them, slaughtering them and their soldiers until they were piled like rotten logs on the ground.

Realising that his troops had been completely defeated, the

Altan Khan fled from Jungdu and made his way to the city of Namging. Those of his soldiers who were left behind were forced to eat human flesh as they starved to death.

Then Chinggis Khan congratulated Tolui and his son-in-law Chugu, saying: 'You have done well.' And he bestowed his favour upon them.

Afterwards Chinggis Khan moved his camp from Qoshiwu to the Shira steppe of Jungdu. Jebe, meanwhile, had stormed the Chabchiyal pass and forced the soldiers who were guarding it to retreat. He returned to his chief. Meanwhile the Altan Khan, before he left, appointed Qada as vice-regent, and it was from him that Chinggis Khan demanded an inventory of all the gold, silver, satins and other goods that were in the city. Onggur, Arqai-qasar and Shigi-qutuqu were sent ahead to take possession of it, and Qada came out to meet them face to face, bringing with him gold and patterned satins.

Then Shigi-qutuqu said: 'Before this, Jungdu and Jungdu's riches belonged to the Altan Khan. Now, by right of conquest, Jungdu and its riches belong to Chinggis Khan. How can you steal from him by offering us satins behind his back? I shall not take them.'

Shigi-qutuqu refused to take anything, but Onggur and Arqai accepted some of the satins. Then they made an inventory of all Jungdu's goods and chattels, and returned to camp.

'What did Qada give you?' asked Chinggis Khan.

And Shigi-qutuqu replied: 'He brought us gold and patterned satins and tried to give them to us. I told him: "Before this, everything in Jungdu belonged to the Altan Khan, now it belongs to Chinggis Khan. How can you steal his goods and offer them to us behind his back?" I refused to accept the satins, but both Onggur and Arqai accepted them.'

Then Chinggis Khan reprimanded Onggur and Arqai sternly, but to Shigi-qutuqu he said: 'You remembered the great principle of obedience.' And he bestowed favour on him, saying: 'Will you be my seeing eyes, my hearing ears?'

When the Altan Khan finally reached Namging, he submitted and abased himself. He sent his own son, Tenggeri, to Chinggis Khan with a hundred companions to be his sentries. When he saw that the Altan Khan had been subjugated,

Chinggis Khan said: 'We will withdraw,' and they turned back. As they negotiated the Chabchiyal pass, Chinggis sent Qasar, at the head of the left flank of his army, along the edge of the sea. 'Set up camp outside the northern capital of Jungdu,' he commanded, 'and make sure they submit. Then continue through the territory belonging to Wuganu of the Jurchet. If Wuganu proves mettlesome, attack him. If he submits, go on through the border cities and along the banks of the Ula and Na'u rivers. Cross the Tawur river upstream and join me at the main base camp.'

He sent three other commanders with Qasar — Jurchedei, Alchi and Tolun. Together they brought Jungdu to its knees, forcing Wuganu to submit, and all the cities in their path were subjugated. Then Qasar led his men upstream along the Tawar river and back to the main base camp.

Years passed, but one day Chinggis Khan heard that a hundred of his emissaries, with Uquna at their head, had been ambushed and killed by the Sarta'ul people.

'How can the "Golden Reins" of my authority be slashed in this way?' he asked.

> 'For vengeance,
> for revenge,

let us ride out against the Sarta'ul people and avenge the deaths of Uquna and my hundred messengers.'

But just as he was about to ride out, Lady Yisui petitioned him, saying:

'My khan,

> you think to cross high ridges,
> ford wide rivers,
> fight distant campaigns,
> and pacify your many nations.

But no creature is born immortal.

> When your body
> like a withered tree
> comes crashing down,

to whom will you entrust
the tangled hemp of your people?
When your body,
like the stone base of a pillar,
crumbles and falls,
to whom will you entrust
this flock of red-polls, your people?

In which of your four steeds, the sons who were born to you, will you put your trust? Your sons, your younger brothers, your people, even my unworthy self, have realised that a choice must be made. The decision is yours.'

Chinggis Khan answered her with a decree:

'Though she is merely a woman of noble blood, Yisui's words are beyond reproach. It hasn't occurred to any of the rest of you to come forward with such a petition; and I,

having no precedent to follow,
forgot myself,
having no fear of death,
became complacent.

Jochi is my eldest son. What do you say?'

But before Jochi could utter a word Cha'adai spoke up: 'Are you asking Jochi to speak because you intend to name him as your successor? How could we let ourselves be governed by a Merkit foundling?'

Then Jochi leapt to his feet and seized Cha'adai's collar.

'The khan our father has never said that I was any different from the rest of you,' he said. 'Why do you discriminate against me? What makes you think you're superior to me? Perhaps you're my superior in stupidity! But if you can beat me in long-distance shooting, I'll cut off my thumb and throw it away. If you can wrestle me to the ground, I swear I'll never rise again from the place where I fall. Let my father decide the matter!'

As Jochi and Cha'adai stood there, holding each other's collars, with Bo'orchu pulling on Jochi's arm and Muqali restraining Cha'adai, Chinggis Khan listened in silence.

Then Koko-chos, who was standing on the left, said: 'Why

Chinggis Khan and two of his sons:
' "I shall pitch many more camps and set you up to rule
in different lands. Thus I separate you" ' (*page 143*)

Chinggis Khan's funeral: 'On the 12th day of
the 7th lunar month in the Year of the Pig, 1227,
he died and was taken up to Heaven' (*page 153–4*)

be in such a hurry, Cha'adai? Of all your father's sons, it was of you that he had the greatest expectations. Sons were born before you:

> the starry Heavens turned once,
> and people fought without pausing for sleep,
> taking each other by surprise.
> The surface of the globe was rolling,
> and people fought without sleeping beneath their
>   quilts.
> They behaved without shame.
> At such a time
> your mother joined the Merkit,
> not wanting to
> but doing it.
> At such a time
> enemies were encountered
> and people ran away,
> not wanting to
> but doing it.
> At such a time
> people were fighting each other,
> at such a time
> people were killing each other,
> not wanting to
> but doing it.

If you talk like that you will harden the heart of butter in your wise mother, you will sour her heart of milk.

> In that warmth
> were you not accidentally
> born from the same belly?
> In that heat
> did you not accidentally
> come from a single womb?
> If your mother,
> who bore you from her heart,
> has cause to be ashamed
> her love will cool,

and when you try to soothe her
it will not work.
If your mother,
who bore you from her belly,
has cause to grumble,
her pain will grow,
and when you try to soothe her,
it will not work.
When the khan your father
forged an entire nation,
he tied his black head to the saddle-strap,
he poured his black blood into a flask;
his black eyes never blinked,
his ear lay flat upon no pillow,
his sleeves became his pillow,
his spread skirts were his mattress,
he drank his own saliva
and caught meat in his teeth at night.

He struggled forward until the sweat of his brow had reached
the soles of his feet, and the sweat from his soles had soaked
up to his brow. And as he forged on, your mother endured at
his side.

Wearing her high hat proudly,
shortening her skirts with a sash,
wearing her high hat tightly,
wrapping her skirt sash firmly,
she reared her sons.
Whenever she swallowed
she gave you half her food.
When her throat was choking
she gave you all of it,
and went hungry.
Pulling you up by the shoulders,
she strove to make you
the equal of other men.
Pulling you up by your necks,
she strove to make you
the equal of other men.

> Cleaning your bodies
> and making you lift your heels,
> she forced you to reach to men's shoulders,
> to the rumps of geldings.

Don't you believe she wants the best for you now? Our wise lady had a heart

> as bright as the sun,
> as wide as a lake.'

At last Chinggis Khan found his voice, and spoke to Cha'adai: 'How dare you speak about Jochi like that? Jochi is my eldest son. Never speak of him like that again.'

But Cha'adai smiled and said: 'I don't want to question Jochi's strength or his intelligence.

> Game killed by tongues
> cannot be carried away.
> Game slain by words
> cannot be skinned.

Jochi and I are your eldest sons. We want to serve our father in partnership with one another. Then let the one who shirks his task be slit open; let the one who lags behind have his heels slashed. Ogodei is the peaceful one — let him be your choice. Ogodei is close to you: you can school him in the mysteries of the Great Hat,* the duties and obligations of khan-ship. He will be a more appropriate choice.'

'What do you say, Jochi?' asked Chinggis Khan. 'Speak!'

'Cha'adai has already spoken for me,' said Jochi. 'We want to serve you in partnership with one another. Let Ogodei be your choice.'

So Chinggis Khan issued a decree. 'Why should you commit yourselves to a partnership?' he asked. 'Mother Earth is wide and her waters and rivers are many. I shall pitch many more camps and set you up to rule in different lands. Thus I shall separate you.'

And he said to them:

---

* The Great Hat was the symbol of the khan's authority.

'Keep your word.
Don't let yourselves be laughed at.
Don't let yourselves be ridiculed.

Altan and Quchar both promised much in the past, but they
failed to keep their promises. What could I do? Remember
what became of them. I shall divide some of Altan and Quchar's descendants between you, as a reminder to you to keep
your word. Now, Ogodei,' he said, 'what do you have to say?
Speak!'

'My khan commands me to speak,' replied Ogodei, 'but
what can I say? I cannot refuse my khan. I can only promise
to be as steadfast as I can. Later, there may be some among
my descendants

> whom the cow would not eat
> though they were wrapped in sedge,
> the dog would not eat
> though they were wrapped in fat.

They might be so unskilled as to miss an elk broadside on,
never mind a rat from behind. I cannot promise more than
this.'

Then Chinggis Khan said: 'If this is Ogodei's answer it will
do. What do you say, Tolui? Speak!'

'The khan our father has named my elder brother,' answered Tolui. 'I shall be at his side,

> his faithful companion,
> reminding him of things he has forgotten,
> waking him when he has slept his fill.
> I shall be the whip of his chestnut gelding,
> the instrument of his obedience,
> never breaking ranks,
> campaigning for him
> wherever I am sent,
> and fighting for him
> in close combat.'

Chinggis Khan heartily approved of Tolui's pledge, and issued
a decree, saying:

'Let one of Qasar's descendants govern. Let one of Alchi-dai's descendants govern. Let one of Otchigin's descendants govern. Let one of Belgutei's descendants govern. So shall the entire Mongol nation be governed. If you pursue this course, accepting one of my descendants as supreme governor — above all, if you do not seek to break or change my decree — you cannot do wrong. Some of Ogodei's descendants may be born so that

> a cow would not eat them
> though they were wrapped in sedge,
> a dog would not eat them
> though they were wrapped in fat,

but surely one of them will be born good?'

So he decreed.

When he rode out to battle he sent messengers to Burqan of the Tangqut people.

'You promised to be my right hand,' he said. 'Now the Sarta'ul people have presumed to cut my Golden Reins, and I must ride out and challenge them. Ride out with me as the right hand of my army.'

Burqan received this message, but before he could say a word Asha-gambu said: 'Since his might appears to be impotent, it is difficult to see how he ever became khan.' He refused to provide the extra soldiers and sent back boastful messages to Chinggis Khan.

Chinggis Khan was furious. 'How can I allow them to speak to me like that?' he asked himself. 'Perhaps I should send some of my men on a detour to teach them a lesson. What difficulties might I then encounter?' Then he made up his mind. 'We are intent on a different people at the moment,' he said. 'That is enough. If Eternal Heaven spares me, then when I return I shall pull firmly on my Golden Reins and settle this other business.'

Chinggis Khan rode out against the Sarta'ul people in 1219, the Year of the Hare. He crossed the Arai, taking from among his women Lady Qulan to keep him company on the campaign.

From among his younger brothers he chose Otchigin* and put him in charge of the main base camp in his absence. Then he sent Jebe ahead in the vanguard, with Sube'etei to back him up. Behind them went Toquchar. All three commanders were given instructions to skirt round the Soltan's army until they reached the far side.

'Wait for us then,' said Chinggis Khan, 'and we will mount a joint attack.'

Jebe skirted the cities of Khan Melik without touching them, and Sube'etei passed them by in the same way. But Toquchar, coming up behind them, could not resist raiding Khan Melik's border towns and plundering his farmers. As a result, Khan Melik turned his back on us and went over to Jalaldin-soltan's side. Together they rode out against Chinggis Khan.

Shigi-qutuqu was in command of the vanguard, but Jalaldin and Khan Melik overcame him and pressed on towards Chinggis Khan himself. But Jebe, Sube'etei and Toquchar came up behind the enemy, overcame them, and slaughtered them. After that, ensuring that the cities of Bukhara, Samarkand and Utrar had no time to unite against him, Chinggis pursued Jalaldin and Khan Melik as far as the Indus river, where many of their soldiers were drowned. The two leaders, however, managed to save their own skins and escaped upstream. Chinggis Khan followed them, plundering Badakhshan, the city of precious stones, on the way. When he reached the confluence of the streams known as the 'Mother' and the 'Mare', he pitched his camp on the Baru'an steppe. Bala of the Jalayir pressed on in pursuit of the fugitives, but Chinggis Khan stayed to bestow his favour on Jebe and Sube'etei.

'Jebe,' said he, 'you were born Jirqo'adai, but when you left the Tayyichi'ut tribe you became Jebe. Toquchar, on the other hand, raided Khan Melik's border cities against my will and turned him against me. I shall have him executed.'

He calmed down, however, and instead of executing Toquchar he reprimanded him sternly, punishing him and demoting him from his command.

---

* Also called Temuge.

When he returned from the Bara'un steppe, Chinggis Khan spoke to three of his sons, Jochi, Cha'adai and Ogodei.

'Take the right flank of my army,' he said, 'cross the Amu river, and set up camp at the city of Urunggechi.'

To Tolui, his fourth son, he said: 'Pitch your camps at Marv, Nishapur and other neighbouring towns.'

He himself set up his camp outside the city of Otarar.

When Jochi, Cha'adai and Ogodei arrived at Urunggechi they sent a petition back to their father. 'Our soldiers are ready and waiting,' they said. 'Which of us shall give the commands?'

And Chinggis answered them with a decree, saying: 'Do as Ogodei tells you.'

He himself brought the city of Otarar into submission, before moving first to Samarkand and then to Bukhara. While he waited for Bala, Chinggis went up to the ridge of Altan-qorqan to pitch his camp in the summer quarters of the Soltan. From there he sent messengers to Tolui, saying:

'The hot season is upon us. The other soldiers are setting up their camps. Come and join us.'

Tolui had already taken Marv, Nishapur and other neighbouring cities, and he was on the point of attacking Herat when he got Chinggis's message. He stormed the city and then returned to his father's camp.

Jochi, Cha'adai and Ogodei, meanwhile, had brought Urunggechi to its knees. They divided the people of the city between them, but did not set aside a share for their father. When they returned and dismounted, Chinggis Khan reprimanded them and refused to give them an audience for three days.

In the end Bo'orchu, Muqali and Shigi-qutuqu petitioned him and said: 'We brought down the Soltan of the Sarta'ul people who had resentfully opposed you, and we took his people and cities. Urunggechi was taken by your sons who divided its spoils among themselves, even though they rightfully belonged to you.

'Heaven and Earth increased our strength and gave us the victory over the Sarta'ul people. Look: your men and geldings are busy and happy as a result. Why should my khan be

angry? Your sons know they have done wrong and are afraid.
Let it be a lesson for the future. Otherwise we fear that your
sons' characters will suffer. Why not show them your favour
and give them an audience? Wouldn't that solve the problem?'

After this Chinggis Khan relented and gave an audience to
his three sons. He reprimanded them, citing

> the words of old men,
> the words of the ancients,

until they almost sank into the ground where they stood, and
had not even enough strength to wipe the sweat from their
brows.

Chinggis Khan hoped to teach them a lesson by scolding
them thoroughly, but three of his quiver-bearers went to him
and remonstrated with him, saying:

'Your sons are like three young falcons learning to hunt.
Why are you so hard on them? They are frightened and
disheartened, and we fear the effect of ignoring their needs.
Our enemies stretch from where the sun sets to where it rises.
When you provoke us — your huge sheep-dogs — to action,
and send us out against the enemy, Heaven and Earth increase
our strength. Our one desire is to return to you with gold and
silver, satin and other goods, men and kinsmen. If you ask
who are your enemies, we say: "Look at Qalibai-soltan of the
Baghdad over in the west. Go and do battle with him!"'

When he heard their petition, Chinggis's anger against his
sons evaporated. He approved the wisdom of his three quiver-
bearers, and issued a decree favouring them: two he kept at
his side, and the third, Chormaqan of the Oteged, he sent out
to wage war on Qalibai-soltan and the Baghdad people.

Dorbei-doqshin was sent to attack the cities of Herat, Marv
and Abtu which lay between the Baghdad people and the
land of the Hindus; while Sube'etei was sent northwards to
wage war on eleven tribes — the Kanglin, Kibcha'ut, Bajigit,
Orusut, Majarat, Asut, Sasut, Serkesut, Keshimir, Bolar and
the Kerel. Chinggis Khan then crossed the great waters of the
Volga and Ural rivers, sending Sube'etei even further ahead,
to the very walls of the wooden city of Kiev.

When he had completed his conquest of the Sarta'ul tribe,

Chinggis Khan issued a decree placing resident commanders in all the various cities. From Urunggechi came a father and son, Yalawachi and Masqut, who told Chinggis all about the customs and laws of the city. When he discovered how much they knew, Chinggis appointed Masqut to join the other resident commanders in governing the cities in the area. Yalawachi he brought back to Jungdu and put him in charge. He did this because the two men were so knowledgeable about the laws and customs of the land.

Chinggis Khan spent seven years in the land of the Sarta'ul, awaiting the return of Bala. He, meanwhile, had crossed the Indus river and pursued Jalaldin and Khan Melik as far as the Hindu border. There he lost them, and though he penetrated right into the heart of Hindu territory, he could not find them. So he turned round and returned to Chinggis's camp, plundering the border towns on the way, and taking many camels and castrated goats with him.

Chinggis Khan then began the long journey back to his own country, spending the summer by the Erdish river on the way. In the autumn of the seventh year,* in the Year of the Cock, 1225, he finally pitched his camp at the Tu'ula palaces in the Black forest.

---

* In fact, the sixth year.

CHAPTER TWELVE
The death of Chinggis Khan and the reign of Ogodei.

CHINGGIS KHAN SPENT THE WINTER IN THE BLACK forest, and during that time he decided to mount a campaign against the Tangqut people. He counted his soldiers afresh, and in the autumn of the Year of the Dog, 1226,* he rode out. From among his wives he chose Lady Yisui to accompany him.

On the way, Chinggis, mounted on his reddish-grey horse, Josotu-boro, hunted the wild horses of the Arbuqa. Once, when the wild horses charged them, Josotu-boro shied, throwing his rider. Chinggis Khan was badly bruised and it was decided to set up camp on the spot, at Cho'orqat. The following morning Lady Yisui called the lords and princes together and said:

'You must decide what to do. The khan is hot with fever, his flesh burns.'

When they were all assembled, Tolun-cherbi of the Qongqa-tad made a suggestion:

> 'The Tangqut people
> have solid camps
> and established cities,'

he said. 'They won't run away with their cities on their backs, deserting their camps. Let us withdraw, and once the khan's fever has subsided we will ride out against them.'

When they heard these words all the lords and princes approved of them and petitioned Chinggis Khan to withdraw. But the khan said:

'The Tangqut people will say our hearts have failed us and we have turned back. We should send a messenger to them, and meanwhile we should pitch our camp here and nurse my

* In fact 1225, as the Mongols were already at war with the Tangqut in 1226.

illness on the spot. Once we have their reply we can decide whether to withdraw or not.'

So he sent an emissary to convey the following message to the Tangqut people:

'Last year, you, Burqan, said you wanted your people to be the right hand of my army. But when I sent a message asking for your help, saying: "The Sarta'ul people will not unite with us—let us ride out against them together," you, Burqan, broke your word and refused to give me your soldiers. Instead you came and mocked me.

'I had other matters to occupy me then, but I swore that when I could I would take up the challenge. I waged war on the Sarta'ul people, and because the Almighty Spirits protected me I brought them into submission. Now I intend to take up the challenge you threw down.'

When he heard Chinggis's message, Burqan said: 'I did not mock him,' and Asha-gambu answered: 'No, I was the one who mocked him. By now, perhaps, the Mongols have learned how to fight. Well, I have a camp in the Alashai

with latticed yurts
and laden camels.

If you dare, come to me there and we will do battle together. If, however, you prefer gold and silver, satins and other goods, then go to the rich cities, go to Eriqaya and Eri-je'u and plunder them.'

So saying, Asha-gambu sent the emissary back. He delivered his message to Chinggis Khan, whose flesh was still hot with fever.

'This is too much,' he said. 'How can I withdraw now, in the face of such boasting? I must punish his braggart words now, even if I die. Let us go.'

And he added: 'Let the Almighty Spirits take command.'

Immediately Chinggis Khan and his army headed out towards Alashai and rode straight into battle with Asha-gambu. The latter was forced to retreat and barricade himself on the mountain, but Chinggis Khan pursued him, finished him off and slaughtered his people

> with their latticed yurts
> and their laden camels

until they blew like ashes in the wind.

Then he issued a decree:

'The Tangqut are a powerful, good and courageous people, but they are fickle. Slaughter them and take what you need to give to the army.'

That summer Chinggis Khan pitched his camp on the Snowy mountain. He sent soldiers out against those of the Tangqut people who had rebelled against him and had climbed the mountain with Asha-gambu, those

> who had latticed yurts
> and laden camels.

The whole tribe was completely wiped out. Then he showed favour to Bo'orchu and Muqali, saying: 'Take what you want, until you can carry no more.'

So he decreed. And he added: 'Because I didn't give you any of the Kitat people, I now give you the Juyin clan to divide equally between you. Make their fine sons follow behind you, holding your falcons. Bring up their daughters to arrange your wives' skirts. The Qara-kitad Juyin were the trusted intimates of the Altan Khan. They were the ones who destroyed the fathers and forefathers of the Mongols. Now, Bo'orchu and Muqali, you two are my trusted intimates.'

So he decreed.

Later Chinggis Khan moved out from the Snowy mountain. First he pitched his camp in Uraqai city and then moved on to Dormegei. While he was breaking up that city, Burqan came to seek an audience with him.

He presented Chinggis Khan with many gifts. First came golden images of the Buddha, then bowls and vessels of gold and silver, nine of each. They were followed by nine boys and girls, nine geldings and nine camels. All kinds of gifts, arranged in sets of nine by kind or colour, were presented to him during that audience, though Chinggis Khan insisted that

Burqan remain outside the felt door of his tent throughout.*
He found it almost impossible to quell his revulsion, and on
the third day he issued a decree changing Burqan's name to
Shidurqu, which means 'loyal'.

Then Chinggis Khan called Tolun-cherbi to him.

'Now we have ensured his loyalty,' he said, 'lay hands on
Shidurqu and kill him.'

Soon afterwards Tolun-cherbi came to him with the news
that he had done as Chinggis had ordered and suffocated his
old enemy.

Then Chinggis Khan issued a decree, saying:

'When I came to the Tangqut to take up their rebellious
challenge, and when my flesh was bruised from hunting
the wild horses of Arbuqa, it was Tolun who said: "Give
his wounds time to heal." He was concerned for my body
and my life, and gave good advice. But we were driven on
by the poisonous words of our enemy and looked for our
strength to the Almighty Spirits. We took our revenge and
brought them down. Tolun shall have all the presents that
Iluqa-burqan brought—the mobile palace, the bowls, the
vessels, everything.'

So he decreed.

By plundering the Tangqut people, by making their leader
change his name before he suffocated him, Chinggis Khan
destroyed the mothers and fathers of the Tangqut even to the
seed of their seed, until they were no more.

Then he issued a decree, saying:

'While we eat, we will talk of our victory, how we finished
them off and saw them die. And we will say to ourselves:
"That is the end. They are no more."'

Because the Tangqut people made promises they did not
keep, Chinggis Khan had hunted them down a second time.
On his return, on the 12th day of the 7th lunar month in the
Year of the Pig, 1227, he died and was taken up to Heaven,

* Recent research indicates that by the time this audience took place
Chinggis Khan was already dead. If so, keeping the Burqan outside
the felt door would have prevented him knowing the truth. (See
Chinggis Qahan-nu Tobchiyan by Saishiyal, Inner Mongolian People's Publishing House, 1987.)

and many of the Tangqut slaves were given to the Lady
Yisui.

In 1228, the Year of the Rat, Cha'adai, Batu and other princes
of the right; Otchigin-noyan, Yegu, Yisungge and other
princes of the left; Tolui and the princes of the centre; the
princesses, the sons-in-law and all the commanders assembled
at Kode'u Aral on the Kerulen river.

There, in accordance with Chinggis Khan's decree, they
named Ogodei as his successor.

Afterwards, Cha'adai and Tolui, his elder and younger
brothers, handed over to Ogodei all those who had guarded
the golden life of their father – the night-guards, the quiver-
bearers, the eight thousand sentries and all the ten thousand
personal servants who had served at the side of my father the
khan.* They also bestowed on him the central heartland of
the Mongolian nation.

The first thing Ogodei Khan did, after he had been raised
to the throne and had assigned all the guards who had served
in the palace, was to consult Cha'adai.

Oqotur and Monggetu were sent out with a contingent of
soldiers to strengthen Chormaqan-qorchi's rearguard in the
campaign against Qalibai-soltan—for Chinggis Khan had
not yet succeeded in subduing the Baghdad tribe.

Sube'etei, meanwhile, was campaigning against the cities
of Meket Men-kermen, Keyibe and others, and, having crossed the Adil and Jayaq rivers, had penetrated as far as the
lands of the Kanglin, Kibcha'ut, Bajigit, Orusut, Asut, Sesut,
Majar, Keshimir, Sergesut, Buqar and Kerel peoples. Now he
found himself in difficulties, and Ogodei Khan sent Batu,
Buri, Guyuk, Mongge and many other princes out to reinforce
his rearguard.

'Batu shall be in overall command of the princes who are
taking part in the campaign,' he decreed, and added: 'Guyuk
shall command those from the central army.'

Then he said: 'Let all those princes who are in charge of a
domain send their eldest sons to join the campaign. Fur-

---

* The author is expressing his personal feelings for Chinggis Khan.

thermore, those princes who have no domain, and the commanders over every contingent whether large or small, shall
also send their eldest sons. Let the princesses and the imperial
sons-in-law send their eldest sons too.'

After he had issued this decree, Ogodei added: 'This principle of sending the eldest sons to join the campaign was
suggested by my elder brother Cha'adai. He sent me word,
saying: "I have sent Buri, my eldest son, to campaign in
Sube'etei's rearguard. If everyone does the same, morale will
be high and the army will be immeasurably strengthened. Out
there beyond our borders are many hostile countries, and
beyond them are people who would die by their own hands
rather than submit. It is said that their weapons are sharp."
This is the message that Cha'adai sent me.'

Then Ogodei said: 'Let us take my elder brother's advice,
follow his zealous example, send out our eldest sons to
fight.'

He proclaimed this decree far and wide, and sent out Batu,
Buri, Guyuk, Mongge and other princes in support.

Then Ogodei sent further word to Cha'adai, asking for
advice.

'Now I am sitting on the throne prepared by our father
Chinggis Khan,' he said, 'but others may well say: "By what
right, by what skills, have you deserved that throne?" Elder
brother Cha'adai, if you approve, I will ride out against the
Kitat people and finish the job that our father began.'

When he heard Ogodei's message, Cha'adai approved
heartily, saying: 'What can go wrong? Appoint someone trust-
worthy to oversee your base camp and ride out. I will select
soldiers from here to support you.'

So Ogodei appointed Oldaqar-qorchi to take command of
the great palace-yurts, and he rode out. He went to war with
the Kitat people in the Year of the Hare, 1231. Jebe was sent
ahead in the vanguard and together they overcame the Kitat
soldiers, slaughtering them until their corpses were piled up
like rotten logs.

Crossing the Chabchiyal, Ogodei sent soldiers in all directions to surround and subdue Kitat towns and cities. He
pitched his camp at Shira-dektur, and there he was struck

down with an illness which deprived him of the use of his tongue and caused him great distress.

Various shamans and soothsayers were called to him, and they divined his illness, and said: 'The spirit lords of the lands and waters belonging to the Kitat people have taken violent possession of the khan because he has ravaged and plundered their towns and cities.' They suggested that gold and silver, livestock and food, even people, might be offered as a substitute for the khan himself, but the spirits refused to leave his body and raged violently inside him. Finally the shamans suggested offering a kinsman as a substitute and suddenly the khan opened his eyes and asked for a drink of water.

'What happened?' he asked, after he had quenched his thirst.

And the shamans answered: 'The spirit lords of the Kitat took possession of you because you had plundered their lands, their waters and their people. They were raging violently against you. When we divined the problem and asked what substitute we should offer, you suffered violent cramps, but when we said: "Would a kinsman be acceptable?" they released their hold on you. Now we leave you to decree the solution.'

When they had petitioned him, Ogodei issued a decree, saying: 'Who among my princes is beside me?'

Then Prince Tolui, who stood beside him, spoke up:

'In spite of your having elder brothers and younger brothers, our fortunate father, Chinggis Khan, chose you to be khan after him. He chose you as one would choose a gelding, as one would examine a wether. Pointing you towards his great throne, he placed upon you the burden of many peoples. As for me, destined to be at the right hand of my elder brother, I was told to serve you by

> reminding you of things you had forgotten
> and waking you when you had slept your fill.

Now, my brother, if I should lose you, whom should I remind of forgotten things, and whom should I rouse from sleep? If the khan my brother dies

Ogodei Khan

the Mongol people will be orphaned,
the Kitat people will have their revenge.

I will take your place:

> I have, in my time,
> split the trout's back,
> I have sliced the sturgeon.
> Ile* I overcame
> and Qada* I impaled.
> My face is handsome
> and my back is long.

Shamans, perform your spells and swear your oaths.'

When the shamans had sworn their oaths, Prince Tolui drank the oath-taking liquid. There he sat, and after a short while he said: 'It has made me drunk. Until I wake from my drunkenness, I leave it to you, my khan, my brother, to look after your orphaned younger brothers, your widowed sister-in-law, until they are all grown up and have achieved intelligence and character. I have said all I wish to say. I am drunk.'

With these words Prince Tolui left the palace-tent, and went away to die.

So Ogodei, after he had defeated Altan Khan, renamed him Se'use, which means 'page'. After plundering the Kitat of their silver and gold, their golden and patterned satins and their other goods, their piebald horses and their pages, Ogodei appointed scouts and garrison commanders. He set up resident commanders in Namging, Jungdu and other strategic cities before returning peacefully in 1232 to set up his own camp at Qara-qorum.†

Chormaqan-qorchi, meanwhile, had subdued the Baghdad people.

Ogodei knew that the land was said to be good and its possessions fine, so he issued a decree, saying:

'Chormaqan-qorchi shall stay in that country as garrison

---

* Ile and Qada were two generals of the Jin dynasty (see p. 137).
† The capital city of Mongolia was in fact built later, in 1235–6.

commander, and every year the people will bring him tributes: yellow gold, gilt, gold brocades and damasks, pearls both large and small, sleek Arab horses with long necks and legs, dull brown workhorses, camels and small-humped camels, pack mules and mules for riding. All this shall Chormaqan-qorchi send to me.'

Batu, Buri, Guyuk, Mongge and the other princes who had been campaigning in the rearguard of Sube'etei-ba'atur's army, also brought the peoples of Kanglin, Kibcha'ud and Bajigid into submission. They crossed the Volga and Ural rivers to attack the city of Meget, where they fell upon the Orusut people and slaughtered them until the tribe was wiped out. They plundered the people of Asut, Sesut, Bolar, Man-kerman, Kiwa and many other cities, forcing them to surrender and appointing resident and garrison commanders to keep them in submission. Finally they returned.

Then Ogodei sent Yisuder-qorchi to reinforce Jalayirtai-qorchi in his campaign against the Jurchet and the Solongqas tribes, and he sent instructions that Yisuder should remain there as garrison commander once they had been subdued.

From the Kibchaq campaign Batu sent one of his messengers to Ogodei Khan with a petition:

'By the strength of Eternal Heaven and the fortune invested in the khan my uncle, I have destroyed the city of Meget, plundered the Orusut tribe, and brought eleven countries and their peoples into submission. Pulling in our Golden Reins, we decided to hold a feast before returning home. We erected a vast tent, and, being the most senior among the princes who were there, I was the first to drink one of the two ceremonial bowls of wine. Buri and Guyuk took exception to this. They refused to join in the feast and rode off. As they went I heard Buri say:

' "Why did Batu drink first, when we are supposed to be his equals?

> When old women with beards
> become our equals
> we should spurn them with our heels
> and trample them with our feet."

And Guyuk said: "These old women with quivers! We should beat their breasts with sticks!"

'To which Eljigidei's son Harqasun added: "We should stick wooden tails on them, so they would beat themselves!"

'So while the rest of us, who had ridden out against those rebellious foreigners, were discussing the campaign and whether or not it had been properly conducted, we had to listen to words like these from Buri and Guyuk. We parted without making up the quarrel, and now I must leave it to my uncle the khan to decide the matter.'

This was the petition he sent to Ogodei Khan.

When he heard Batu's petition, Ogodei was very angry indeed, and he refused Guyuk an audience.

'Who is inciting this lowly prince,' he demanded, 'who has made him think he can insult his superiors in this way? Let him rot by himself like an egg! He was always antagonistic towards Batu in spite of Batu's seniority:

> I shall make him a scout —
> he shall climb
> city walls like mountains
> until his ten fingernails drop off;
> I shall make him commander
> of a garrison, to climb
> the hard-packed city walls
> until his five fingernails splinter.

As for you, Harqasun, wicked, lowly and petty as you are, who were you imitating when you insulted your superior with your boastful words? I would have you executed, but you would argue that I was prejudiced in Guyuk's favour. Instead, I exile you both.

'As for Buri, Batu shall send him to my elder brother Cha'adai to repeat what he has said. Let elder brother Cha'adai decide on the matter!'

Then Mongge, son of Tolui and a future khan, spoke up on behalf of the princes, while Alchidai, Qongqortai and Janggi spoke for the lords. This was the advice they presented to Ogodei Khan:

'Your father decreed that matters arising in the field should only be judged in the field, while domestic matters should only be judged at home. The khan is angry with Guyuk, but this is really a field matter and should be dealt with on the spot. If the khan favours us, would it not be better to send Guyuk to Batu and rely on his judgement?'

When he heard their petition, Ogodei approved of it and calmed down. He received Guyuk in audience, and reprimanded him, saying:

'It is said of you that during the campaign

> you did not spare the buttocks
> of any man with buttocks.

It is also said of you that

> you broke down the morale
> of every man in the army.

Do you think that your wrath and anger alone were responsible for subjugating the Orusut people? Do you think, in your arrogance, that you alone forced them to submit, and that you now have the right to insult a man who is your senior? Remember the words decreed by Chinggis Khan, our father. Did he not say:

> "Many people cause one to fear,
> deep waters cause one to die."

You act as if you achieved victory all on your own, but you were sheltered by Sube'etei and Bujek, and all the soldiers in their army helped you to bring the Orusut and Kibcha'ut into submission.

'So you gained an Orusut kinsman or two: you have not yet gained the hoof of a kid before you start flaunting your manhood. You make one journey from your yurt and think you've achieved everything single-handed. Then you come bragging to me. Enough. Mongge, Alchidai, Qongqortai, Janggi and the others,

> being my good companions,
> have stayed my angry heart,

like a large ladle
they have contained my overflowing anger.

Enough, I say! They have told me it is a field matter, to be judged by Batu in the field. I leave you both to him.'

And he sent them away, adding: 'Buri I leave to my elder brother Cha'adai.'

Then Ogodei spoke again:

'This decree newly proclaims the duties of all the guards — the night-guards, quiver-bearers and sentries — who served my father Chinggis Khan before me. Let it be understood that as they served formerly in accordance with my father's wishes, so shall they serve now.'

So he decreed.

And he said: 'All quiver-bearers and sentries shall follow their own paths during the day as they did in former times, and, at sunset, they will yield to the night-guards and spend the night outside.'

So he decreed.

And he said: 'The night-guards shall spend the night with us. Some shall stand at the door and round the yurt, others will patrol in front and behind the palace. After sunset the night-guards will seize anyone who moves near the yurt, and will hold them prisoner until dawn. After the crowds have dispersed, the night-guards will seize any man who tries to enter and mix with them, but is not one of them: they shall split open his head and throw him on one side. If a man comes in the night with an urgent message, let him tell the night-guards, and then, flanked by them at the rear of the yurt, let him report to me. Qongqortai, Suiraqan and others, together with the night-guards, shall be in charge of comings and goings at the palace-yurt. For example, I heard that Eljigidei, in spite of being trusted, was seized by the guards when he tried to walk behind them. Night-guards who are trusted should not countermand my decrees.'

So he decreed.

And he said: 'No one shall ask a night-guard to reveal his number, and no one shall walk behind him at his post. No one shall walk between the night-guards: they have my orders to seize any man who walks either between or behind them. If any man asks a night-guard his number, let the gelding he has ridden that day be taken away from him, together with its saddle and bridle and the clothes he has worn. No one shall sit on the seat of the night-guards, whoever they are. Let the night-guards look after the banners, drums, pikes, spears, bowls and vessels; and let them also organise food and drink and the uncut meat.'

Then he decreed: 'Let the night-guards look after the palace-yurt carts. Unless we are campaigning in person, the night-guards shall not campaign, and while we are at hunting and falconry their numbers will be restricted — half will remain with the palace-yurt cart, and half will go with us. From among the guards, the camp administrators shall go ahead to set up our palace-tent. Some shall stand guard on the door. Qada'an, the commander of one thousand, shall be in overall command of the night-guards.'

So he decreed.

Again he appointed various commanders to be in charge of different shifts, saying: 'Qada'an and Bulaqadar shall consult together and form one shift. They will then direct their men to take up positions to the left and right hand of the palace. Amal and Chanar shall consult together and form a second shift, also directing their men to take up positions on the left- and right-hand sides of the palace. Qadai and Qori'qachar shall do the same with a third shift, and Yalbaq and Qara'udar with a fourth.

'Furthermore, the first two shifts will camp on the left-hand side of the palace and shall operate from that side, while the second two shifts shall camp on the right.'

And he said: 'Let Qada'an take overall charge of all four shifts. Furthermore, the night-guards will stand all round the palace, as close as possible to my person, and shall lie down close to the door. Two among them shall enter the palace and present the kumiss flasks.'

So he decreed.

And again he said: 'The four quiver-bearers, Yisun-to'e, Bugidei, Horqudaq and Lablaqa, shall form separate companies from among their men, and shall organise them into shifts to carry quivers.'

So he decreed.

Furthermore, he appointed elders from among the children of those who had formerly been in charge to oversee the shifts of sentries, saying: 'As Alchidai and Qongqortai were formerly in charge of the sentries, let them now organise one shift together and enter it in my service. Temuder and Jegu shall organise a second shift, and Mangqutai, who was in charge of the rearguard, shall organise a third.'

Again he issued a decree: 'Eljigidei shall be the senior commander and all shall serve according to Eljigidei's commands.'

Again he decreed: 'If a man abandons his shift once he has entered into my service, his commander shall follow my father's rule and teach him a lesson with three strokes of the rod. If the same man abandons his shift for a second time, he shall receive seven strokes of the rod. And if, without the excuse of illness and without consulting his senior officer, he abandons his shift for a third time, he shall receive thirty-seven strokes of the rod and be exiled out of our sight, for he obviously finds it too difficult to serve us properly. Again, if the elders do not register the guards who are serving on the shift, thereby abandoning their duty to their men, we shall punish the elders. Furthermore, the elders in charge should announce this decree to the guards at every third shift at the moment the shifts are changed. If, in spite of having heard the order, the guards abandon their shifts, then by rule of this decree we shall punish them. If the elders do not announce the decree to their men, they shall be found guilty themselves and punished. Furthermore, although the elders are senior to their men, they shall not punish the guards who entered my service with them on an equal footing, without my permission. If any senior breaks this decree, let him be reported to us! If any deserves execution, I shall execute him. If any deserves punishment, I shall punish him. If any senior, merely because he is senior, lays hands on my guards without first reporting to me, he shall be repaid in kind — a rod for a rod, a fist for a fist.'

Then he issued a further decree and said: 'Furthermore, my

guards are higher in rank than the leaders of one thousand beyond the palace walls, and my guards' attendants rank higher than those who command a hundred men or ten. If any commander of one thousand from outside these walls disputes with my guards, we shall punish him!'

Again, Ogodei Khan said: 'I shall not let my people endure what they endured while my father Chinggis Khan was establishing the nation. Instead I shall rest

> their feet upon the earth,
> their hands upon the ground,

and let them rejoice. We sit upon the throne prepared by our father the khan, and we do not wish to see our people suffer. Let everyone give one three-year-old sheep annually from their herds to make my soup. Taking one sheep from every hundred, let them give it to the poor and needy among their fellow soldiers. Furthermore, how can we levy kumiss from people on every occasion when my elder and younger brothers gather together with all their men, geldings and guards? From the various units of one thousand, the men will provide mares, and those who milk the mares shall herd them. The camp organisers shall constantly provide replacement mares, and shall be called "the herders of foals and colts". Again, when my elder and younger brothers gather, I shall give them rewards and gifts. I shall pour satins, silver ingots, quivers, bows, breastplates and weapons into the storehouse and set my men to guard them. I shall select store-keepers and grain-keepers to guard our storehouses. Furthermore, we shall divide up the pasture between the people of the nation. If we choose camp organisers from among the various units of a thousand men and send them to settle the pastures, won't that do? In the Chol desert there are nothing but wild beasts. For the people who live in the wide open spaces, let the camp organisers, headed by Chanai and Ui'urtai, dig wells and fence them in.

'At the moment, our messengers gallop straight through the settlements of the people, thus delaying our official business so that the people of the nation suffer. We shall settle this once and for all by establishing post-stations at various stages on the route, and recruiting post-station keepers and post-horse keepers from among the various units of one thousand men. If we direct our messengers to gallop by way of the post-stations, rather than straight through the settlements of the people (unless, of course, it is urgent), will that not suffice? When Chanai and Bolqadar, who both understand these things, suggested this, I thought they were right, and I said: "Let my elder brother Cha'adai decide. If he thinks the matter has been properly discussed, and he approves, let him make the final decision." When I sent a message to him, he sent a reply, saying: "You have asked my opinion on these matters. I approve of everything. Do what you suggest." And elder brother Cha'adai sent a further message saying: "I will begin to set up post-stations from this end, so that your stations will link up with mine. Furthermore, I will send a messenger to Batu asking him to do the same." And he added a message saying: "Of everything that has been discussed, this idea for the post-stations is the most fitting and important." '

Then Ogodei Khan said: 'Elder brother Cha'adai, Batu and the other princes of the right hand, all my elder and younger brothers, Otchigin-noyan, Yegu and the rest, all the brothers of the left hand, the princes, the princesses and the imperial sons-in-law of the centre, the commanders of ten thousand, one thousand, of a hundred and of ten, have all approved. When they approved they agreed that it was nothing for them to promise a two-year-old wether yearly from their herds to supply soup for the Dalai* Khan. And it is good to provide a sheep from every hundred to give to the poor and needy. When we have established the post-stations and recruited station keepers and post-horse keepers, the people will be able to live peacefully, while the messengers travel with ease. Everyone has approved.'

His elder brother Cha'adai had also approved. From every unit of a thousand all the people provided one wether annually, according to the khan's decree, to make his soup, while one wether from every hundred was set aside to feed the poor and needy. He also had them supply mares, and people to herd the foals and colts. Store-keepers and grain-keepers were

* Dalai means 'sea' or 'ocean', so by extension 'huge' or 'great'.

assigned to the storehouses and post-station keepers and post-horse keepers to the new post-stations. They measured the distance between the various stages on different routes, and established the stations along them. Arajan and Toquchar were put in charge, and at each station there were twenty post-horse keepers, while at each stage in between there were also twenty post-horse keepers.

Then he decreed: 'From where I sit I have fixed the numbers of post-horse geldings, the sheep for provisions, the milch-mares, the oxen to be harnessed to the carts and the carts themselves:

> if even a short string is missing
> I will divide the goods of the thief
> straight down the middle, and prove him guilty.
> If even a spoon-shaped spoke is missing
> I will split the thief down the line of his nose
> and prove him guilty.'

Ogodei Khan said: 'Here I sit upon my father's great throne, and the deeds I have accomplished since my father's death are these: for my first deed, I finished off his campaign against the Jaqut people. For my second, I established post-stations so that our messengers could gallop swiftly on their way and our necessary goods be easily transported. For my third, I had wells dug in places where there was no water, so that water could be brought forth. For my fourth, I placed scouts and garrison commanders among the peoples of the outlying cities in all directions, and I have allowed the people of my nation to rest

> their feet upon the earth,
> their hands upon the ground.

I have let them live again. Thus I have added four deeds to the great deeds of the khan my father. But I must confess that when I was made to sit upon his throne and load myself with the burdens of his people, I let myself be conquered by wine. This was my first fault. My second fault was that I listened thoughtlessly to the words of women, and had all the girls belonging to my father's brother Otchigin brought to me. My third fault was to harm Doqolqu secretly, he who fought valiantly before his rightful master, the khan my father. Who will fight before me now? I blame myself for harming him behind his back, without appreciating him. He was a man who adhered diligently to his principles, both in front of my father the khan and in front of everyone.

'Furthermore, I am greedy, and fearing that the wild beasts, destined for us by Heaven and Earth, would make their way into the lands of my elder and younger brothers, I had walls and fences built. But though I stopped them straying, I heard words of complaint from my elder and younger brothers. This was my fourth fault. So after my father the khan's death, I added four good deeds to his, but I also committed four faults.'

In 1228, the Year of the Rat, in the month of the Roebuck, a great assembly gathered, and, as the palaces were set up at Dolo'an-boldaq of Kode'e Aral on the Kerulen river and Shilginchek, we finished writing this history.

Chinggis Khan's Principal Warriors.

The 'Four Best Geldings'

This was the name given to Chinggis Khan's four great marshals, Muqali, Bo'orchu, Boro'ul and Chila'un-ba'atur. Together with his 'Four Hounds', they were the principal architects of Chinggis's military achievements. The speed and stamina of Mongol horses played a crucial role in establishing the empire, and only geldings were used in battle, hence the name.

MUQALI, or Muqulai (1170–1223) belonged to the Jalayir tribe. He was taken by his father, Gu'un-u'a, to serve under Chinggis Khan, and Gu'un-u'a himself saved Chinggis's life during a battle by giving him his horse. Gu'un-u'a was killed as a result. Muqali grew up to be a warrior of outstanding talent and high courage. He had a 'lion's chest', and an 'elephant's strength', and he was a great archer. In 1206, after Chinggis's elevation to Great Khan, he appointed Muqali as 'Head of Ten Thousand Men of the Left Hand', in addition to his post as head of a thousand men.

In 1218 Muqali was given the title of 'Prince', the highest honour that the khan could confer, in recognition not only of the father's sacrifice but also of the son's enduring loyalty and courage. At around the same time Chinggis decreed that while he would rule over the northern part of the empire (Mongolia), Muqali would rule the south (part of present-day northern China). When he rode out against the Sarta'ul he put his youngest brother Temuge in charge of Mongolia and appointed Muqali to take charge of the occupation of Jin (northern China).

Chinggis Khan praised Muqali in a song:

> 'You are my elephant:
> you charge unhesitating

into wildfire battles.
You are my monument:
   unmoving as stone,
   you bear my standard.
You are my bounteous host —
   at the great feast
   most fit to distribute food.
Through many battles
   you have carried my pike on high
   and frightened my enemies.
Muqali, my prince and my prime minister!'

Bo'orchu was the son of Naqu the Rich of the Arulad tribe. When Chinggis was young and poor, Bo'orchu helped him recover some stolen horses (see Chapter Two), and in 1189, when Chinggis was first made khan, he appointed Bo'orchu as chief of the Royal Life Guards. This was a time of great unrest, and Chinggis only really slept peacefully when Bo'orchu was on guard.

When, in 1199, Chinggis was asked by the Ong Khan for help, he sent his best warriors with Bo'orchu at their head. He also allowed Bo'orchu to borrow his best gelding, 'the Ear', telling him: 'If you want the horse to gallop, don't whip him, just wave your whip over his mane.' Bo'orchu rode into battle, and, forgetting his chief's instructions, whipped the horse, which stopped dead and refused to move. Suddenly Bo'orchu remembered what he had been told, and waved his whip over the horse's mane. 'The Ear' then galloped like lightning and Bo'orchu and his men were victorious.

To Chinggis, Bo'orchu was 'the second shaft of his cart', and as important as one of his own hands. He spent a lifetime's service in the Guards, so did not have the opportunity to establish a distinguished military career; however, he was always at Chinggis's side and was one of the few who was able to placate him when he was angry. Chinggis praised him in song, saying:

   'When I was young
   and searching for my geldings,

we met as the sun was rising,
and since that time
you have served me with your life;
you, son of Naqu the Rich,
my most beloved warrior.

You roam the countryside
as gently as a two-year piebald ox,
but when you go to war
you rage like lions and tigers;
you take no heed for your life
when you face our enemies.

Bo'orchu, my benevolent warrior!

Facing the black foe,
you rage like hawks and falcons,
not sparing the warm breath of life
when you face the foreign foe.

Happy and carefree your nature,
like that of a gentle two-year ox,
but when you encounter the enemy
you rage like the furious beasts,
taking no heed of your body
to defeat the greedy foe.

Bo'orchu, my blessed friend!

At play as friendly
as an autumn foal,
but when you face the foe
you pounce like a hawk or a falcon.

All your life you have served me well,
Bo'orchu, my best friend;
you will follow your khan forever,
Bo'orchu, my beloved warrior.'

BORO'UL was a member of the Jirkin tribe. He was found as
a child by Chinggis's army and adopted by his mother,
Ho'elun. He grew up to be a brave and powerful warrior,

and, as one of Chinggis's 'Four Best Geldings', he took part in all the major battles. He was also entrusted with the important task of preparing the khan's meat and drink.

In 1206, after Chinggis's elevation to Great Khan, Boro'ul was appointed head of a thousand men, and later saved the lives of Chinggis's sons, Tolui and Ogodei. He was killed in action, fighting at Qori-tumet (see Chapter Ten). Chinggis praised him in song, saying:

> 'When the arrows rained on us
> you were my shield;
> at the time of the whistling arrows
> you were my shelter.
> When you were wounded
> you stayed in the saddle —
> Boro'ul, my man amongst men.'

CHILA'UN-BA'ATUR came from the Tayyichi'ut tribe. He, his father, Sorqan-shira, and his brother and sister saved Chinggis's life when he was young (see Chapter Two), and Chinggis never forgot, saying: 'When I was young the Tayyichi'ut brothers hated me and took me prisoner. You, Sorqan-shira, and your three children helped me to escape. I shall remember what you did for me in my days and in my nights, in my sleep and in my rest.'

Chila'un was extremely brave. Once, in battle, he fell from his gelding and, as an enemy general was about to finish him off, leaped to his feet and killed the general instead. At that point Chinggis gave him the title 'ba'atur', meaning 'hero'.

The 'Four Hounds'

These were Chinggis Khan's four great generals, who, with the 'Four Best Geldings', formed the core of Chinggis's conquering army.

JEBE was a famous warrior belonging to the Tayyichi'ut tribe. It was he who admitted to shooting Chinggis's horse from under him (see Chapter Four), but Chinggis was so impressed with his honesty and his skills as an archer that he welcomed him into his army and bestowed on him the name 'Jebe', which means 'arrowhead'. He was appointed head of a thousand men and became one of Chinggis's 'Four Hounds'. When Chinggis attacked the Jin in 1211 Jebe was appointed to lead the vanguard and, in 1213, under his command, the Mongols took the Chabchiyal pass and Dungchang (present-day Mukden). In 1218 Jebe returned from Qara-kitad with a thousand superb white geldings, which he presented to Chinggis as reparation for 'the khan's best gelding, which I shot'. He was also involved in the Kwarizm campaign (1219–25) but died in Kanglin in 1224 on his way home.

SUBE'ETEI (1176–1248) came from the Uriangqad tribe and led the vanguard in Chinggis's battle against the Naiman in 1204. There he proved himself an outstanding military leader, and in 1206 was appointed the head of a thousand men. With Jebe he took part in the Kwarizm campaign (1219–25) and helped to defeat the Russian army which was menacing the European frontiers. Chinggis once said that Sube'etei was never known to dismount from his horse but was always fighting his enemies: he gave him many presents — pearls and silver vases — and in 1224 Sube'etei presented Chinggis with ten thousand superb geldings.

Before the campaign against the Tangqut people in 1225–7 Chinggis decreed that Sube'etei had done enough and should stay behind, but Sube'etei answered: 'While your majesty must work and suffer, it is not proper that I, your minister, should retire. I would rather go with you.' He accompanied Chinggis on the campaign and, when Chinggis died in 1227, he escorted the coffin safely back to Mongolia. He went on to command the vanguard in the European campaign of 1235–42. During this campaign, the Mongols established themselves in Russia as the 'Golden Horde'.

JELME came from the Uriangqad tribe and was given to Chinggis as a servant by his father. He and Bo'orchu were the first to serve Chinggis and, when he became khan in 1189, both were appointed as chiefs of the Royal Life Guards. In

1203, during a battle with the Ong Khan at Qaljid, Chinggis's army was in danger of defeat, but Jelme turned the tables by attacking the Ong Khan's forces from the rear. In 1206 he was made head of a thousand men, but died about five years later. Chinggis praised him the following poem:

> 'You brought me the wild beasts to kill,
> and chilled the hearts of my enemies.
> When I had no horse you brought me one,
> when I had no drink you brought me one.
> Always vigilant,
> you slept lightly, acted wisely,
> serving our nation from its early days,
> you, Jelme, the best, from Uriangqad.'

QUBILAI was a member of the Barulas tribe and, with Chinggis's younger brother Qasar, served from the earliest days as sword-bearer in the Night-Guards. This was one of the most trusted posts. In war Qubilai always served in the vanguard, and in 1206 he was appointed head of a thousand men.

Chinggis said: 'You, Qubilai, with Jebe, Jelme and Sube'etei, are my four furious hounds. I shall always send you ahead as the vanguard, while Bo'orchu, Muqali, Boro'ul and Chila'un serve as my supports. With Jurchedei and Quyildar as my scouts I shall have peace of mind, and henceforth Qubilai shall take charge of military affairs.' After 1211 Qubilai's name does not appear in any known document.

Apart from the 'Four Best Geldings' and the 'Four Hounds', three other prominent warriors deserve mention:

SHIGI-QUTUQU was found as a child by Chinggis's soldiers when they attacked the Tatar tribe, and he was adopted by Chinggis's mother, Ho'elun. He was reputed to be a fine shot. When he was ten years old he went out on a snowy day and returned very late. Chinggis asked him where he had been. He replied that he had chased thirty deer and had killed twenty-seven of them. In 1206 he was appointed Chief Justice and placed in charge of judicial affairs. Chinggis Khan rewarded him as if he had been one of his own brothers.

Mother Ho'elun adopted four children in all, Shigi-qutuqu, Boro'ul, Guchu and Kokochu. Shigi-qutuqu lived to be over ninety, and in Mongolia, if one wanted to wish anyone a long life, it was customary to say: 'Live as long as Shigi-qutuqu.' Chinggis Khan praised him in the following lines:

> 'You befriended the Merkit tribe,
> you troubled the Mongol tribe,
> you recognised the Tayyichi'ut tribe,
> you defeated the enemy.
> You are mine, from the Tatar tribe!'

JURCHEDEI came from the Uru'ut tribe, serving first Jamuqa (a major character in the history) and then Chinggis Khan. In the battle between Ong Khan and Chinggis, Jurchedei fought bravely and shot superbly, injuring the Ong Khan's son and enabling Chinggis to gain the victory. In 1206 Chinggis appointed Jurchedei head of a thousand men and gave him one of his own wives (see Chapters Six and Eight). Jurchedei died around 1234.

QUYILDAR came from the Mangqut tribe and, like Jurchedei, served Jamuqa first before joining Chinggis Khan's army. When the rest of Quyildar's clan deserted back to Jamuqa, Chinggis questioned Quyildar's decision to stay, at which Quyildar took an arrow from his quiver and broke it in two, saying: 'If I should betray you, I should be like this.' Chinggis praised his wisdom, and they became sworn brothers. Afterwards Chinggis said: 'When Quyildar is with me my mind is at rest.' He was wounded in battle (see Chapter Six) but was almost cured by the best medicine Chinggis could provide. However, he disregarded Chinggis's advice, went hunting, suffered a relapse and died.

The Arts of War
under Chinggis Khan.

During the thirteenth century all Mongols thought themselves to be the centre of the universe, a belief which they derived from their shamanist religion. A shamanist worshipped natural things: the sky, the sun, the moon, rivers and mountains, etc. Heaven was both their guide and their conscience; thus every shamanist was born free and equal. Chinggis was, like any other Mongol, a shamanist, and he treated every Mongol equally.

The Mongols, under Chinggis's command, were united to face the challenges of the time. Their strength lay in their unity, and in the way they deployed their hunting skills and their nomadic economy. Always superb horsemen, their iron discipline, high morale and splendid leadership ensured that as a cavalry force they were beyond compare. Special attention was paid to the welfare of the soldiers. Chinggis Khan once said:

'My soldiers are as numerous as forests, and their women could form a large unit within the army. I want to feed them with juicy meat, let them live in beautiful yurts and let them pasture their livestock on rich soil.'

He was known for his personal concern for the fatigue, hunger and thirst of his men, and was careful not to drive them beyond the limits of their endurance.

Because the population of Mongolia was so small (some say it was over one million; I am inclined to put it at two million), human life was very precious. One can see from Chinggis's tactics that the Mongols tended to avoid hand-to-hand fighting in order to minimise casualties among their soldiers. If a Mongol soldier was killed due to carelessness his commander would be punished for it, and if a wounded Mongol soldier was left on the battlefield his troop leader could be executed on the spot. In December 1241, the

Mongols, under Prince Batu (the founder of the Golden Horde), entered Hungary and fought a major battle on the banks of the Sayo river. Because of the delay in sending rafts to the river banks, some twenty Mongol soldiers lost their lives. Prince Batu strongly reprimanded his second-in-command, the famous general Sube'etei (one of the Four Hounds of Chinggis), for the delay, though some say that Sube'etei and his soldiers arrived late only because they were building bridges over the Sayo.

What is clear is that Chinggis cared very much for his soldiers. With 129,000 Mongol cavalrymen he conducted wars in foreign countries for a period of over twenty years, his golden rule being that of 'loyalty to one another'. Because of the treatment meted out to his troops, he was able to maintain fairly constant numbers of men in his army.

Chinggis and his generals built up an exceptional understanding of the economic, military and political conditions of the countries they wanted to attack through their network of spies, traders and informers. It was said that in the mornings, when the air was at its clearest, a Mongol could see up to four or five miles distant, and could hear the sound of hoofs up to twenty miles away. Even in recent times a horseman could ride from Ulaan-Baatar to Kalgan in nine days — a distance of 600 miles. In 1221 Chinggis's army rode 130 miles from Bamian to Ghazna, via Kabul, in two days. Every man learned to ride from the age of three, and served in the army from the age of fourteen until he was sixty.

Chinggis's Arts of War were based on five key elements:

1. Speed
2. Suddenness
3. Ferocity
4. Variety of Tactics
5. Iron Discipline

Marco Polo tells us that a Mongol cavalryman often slept mounted and armed while his gelding grazed, and that he could go ten days without cooking food. On such occasions he lived on ten pounds of dried milk-curd, two litres of kumiss, and a quantity of cured meat. A Mongol soldier had three or four spare geldings, and would not ride a gelding until it had rested for three or four days. The Mongols took their herds of cow and sheep with them when they went away on campaigns. If they went short of food they simply hunted wild beasts.

In 1211, when Chinggis attacked the Jin territory in north China, his army comprised about 110,000 Mongol soldiers. In 1219, when the Mongol army moved into the Kwarizm territory, the army numbered about 150,000 soldiers (some say only 90,000), but to these he had added many auxiliaries, including Kurds, Turks, Turkomans and even Chinese. Chinggis Khan never liked to fight on a second front unless absolutely necessary, preferring to concentrate his forces on one front at a time.

The Fifteen Military Tactics of Chinggis Khan

1 CROW SOLDIERS AND SCATTERED STARS TACTICS (also known as Ocean Waves Tactics)

When they faced the enemy, the army would split into small groups consisting of three to five soldiers to avoid being surrounded. Chinggis ordered that when the enemy scattered the Mongols should also scatter, and when the enemy regrouped they should also regroup. They were to appear suddenly, like something dropping from the sky, and disappear like lightning. The attack would be signalled by a shout or the crack of a whip. One hundred cavalrymen could surround a thousand enemy soldiers and a thousand cavalrymen could control a front thirty-three miles long in order to attack the enemy at the right place and the right moment (see Chapter Seven).

2 THE CAVALRYMEN CHARGE TACTICS (also known as Chisel Attack Tactics)

A group of cavalrymen would make a direct charge into the enemy line; if the first charge failed, a second and even a third group were to attack. No matter how great the opposition, even if they numbered a hundred thousand, they could not withstand the charges. Finally, in response to a signal, the Mongol cavalrymen would charge from all directions into the enemy lines in order to destroy their formation (see Chapter Seven).

3 Archers' Tactics

The archers, armed with shields, dismounted from their geldings, and shot at the enemy, sometimes using the geldings as ramparts behind which to shelter. Other archers shot from horseback, the horses being trained to stop dead in mid-gallop to allow the archer to take aim. Once the enemy came under fire, their lines would be broken and they would scatter in disorder. At that point the cavalrymen would attack the enemy lines.

4 Throw-into-Disorder Tactics

If the enemy was strong in the battlefield or was sheltering in a fort, so that there was no way to win, the Mongols would herd oxen and wild horses into the enemy lines to cause confusion. These stampede tactics always worked.

5 Wearing-Down Tactics

When the enemy stood in a defensive position with spears planted in rows, thus preventing a cavalry charge into the line, the Mongols would withdraw their main forces, leaving only a few small detachments to harass the enemy by shooting arrows into the spear-held line. Due to lack of food, water and rest, the enemy would eventually have to move. Once the weary forces were on the march, the Mongol army would launch a surprise attack.

6 Confuse and Intimidate Tactics

In 1204, Chinggis Khan ordered his soldiers to set up camp, spreading out over the Sa'ari steppe (in western Mongolia). Every able-bodied man lit five fires some distance apart, which scared the Naiman people and enabled Chinggis Khan to defeat them.

When the Mongols encountered numerically superior

forces, they often sent troops to stir up dust behind their own lines by means of branches tied to the tails of their horses. On seeing this, the enemy sometimes believed that large reinforcements were at hand and fled.

The Mongols also placed stuffed dummies, small Mongol children and females, on the spare horses to suggest that the army was much bigger than it was. This trick was used by the Mongol general Shigi-qutuqu in 1221 when he engaged Jaladin at Biruan between Kabul and Ghazna.

7 LURE-INTO-AN-AMBUSH TACTICS

As soon as battle started, the Mongol soldiers would make a feigned retreat. They deliberately threw away gold and silver and other impedimenta. Such tactics were used sparingly — for example, if they could not break into heavily fortified cities or through a strong pass. In 1211, when the Mongols first attacked the Jin territory in north China, Chinggis Khan sent Jebe and Guyigu Nek as vanguards to attack the famous Chabchiyal pass. The Mongols could not break through this pass because it backed onto mountain cliffs and was strongly fortified. Instead they decided to lure the enemy out by slowly retreating. The Jin army thought that the Mongols had given up, so they chased after them, and were surprised, after riding a certain distance, to see the retreating Mongol soldiers suddenly turn to counter-attack. At that moment, the main Mongol army appeared from all sides in a pre-arranged ambush and slaughtered the enemy until their bodies piled up as far as Chibchiyal like rotten logs. Jebe stormed the gate of Chibchayal, and took the pass (see Chapter Eleven).

In May 1222, the two Mongol generals, Jebe and Sube'etei, and 20,000 Mongol cavalrymen pursued the fleeing Kypchaks (or Cumans) from the west side of the Caspian Sea towards the north-west, to Kiev. The Mongols met the joint forces of the Russians and the Cumans, 30,000 men, on the eastern bank of the Dnieper river. Some say that Sube'etei, with only 2,000 Mongol cavalry, lured the Russians and Cumans for nine days towards the little Kalka river which flows into the Sea of Azov, where the main Mongol cavalrymen numbering 20,000 were waiting. Under the direction of Jebe and

Sube'etei, the Mongols attacked the enemy at the end of May
and destroyed most of their forces.

8 Arc Formation Tactics

The Mongols would send out two detachments in a wide
curve, as in the tips of a bow, but with the main forces staying
at the centre of the arc, hiding in shady places to await the
enemy. These two detachments went first to engage the enemy,
shooting to infuriate them and lure them to the place where
the main forces were waiting. These two detachments also
closed in from the flanks or from behind the enemy. The
Mongols called these tactics 'bow tactics'.

The Cossacks also used these tactics in successfully defeating their enemies.

9 Lightning Attack Tactics and Surprise Attack Tactics

These two tactics were perhaps the most important of all: the
lightning attack meant speed, and the surprise attack meant
suddenness. In 1203, the Mongols attacked Ong Khan, who
had erected a golden yurt and was feasting. For three nights
and three days, under Chinggis's command, they fought, and
in the end Ong Khan and his son managed to escape, though
his entire army surrendered. This was an example of Chinggis's 'surprise attack' tactics. (For details see Chapter Six.)

In 1213, the Mongol army, commanded by Jebe, failed to
take the city of Dungchang (Mukden), so they retreated for
six days over a distance of about 170 miles. The enemy who
were defending the city thought that the Mongols had given
up, but Jebe with his Mongol cavalrymen returned to the city,
covering the distance in one night and launching a surprise
attack. This was an example of 'lightning attack' tactics. (For
details see Chapter Eleven.)

10 Outflanking Tactics

When the Mongol cavalrymen could not attack the enemy
from the front, they would leave a small detachment in front
to draw the attention of the enemy. Meanwhile the main force
went round the back, via almost impassable roads, to attack

the enemy from the rear. There are two examples to illustrate these tactics in the *History*. In 1207, Chinggis Khan ordered Dorbei-doqshin to attack the Tumet people in the northern part of Mongolia. He left a small detachment on the main road, and ordered his best soldiers to travel on the paths made by the red bulls (*sic*: deer). They climbed the highest mountain, then suddenly came down as though descending from Heaven, finishing the enemy while they were feasting.

In 1213, when the Mongol cavalrymen under Chinggis Khan wanted to take Chabchiyal pass, the Jin army fortified it strongly and spread iron spikes on the road to the north to prevent the advance of the geldings. The entrance to the pass was also reinforced by an iron gate. Chinggis left a small detachment to shoot at the Jin army, then took his main army west and back to the southern end of the pass. He captured a place called Nan Kou, and went on to take the pass.

11 ENCIRCLING TACTICS

Chinggis used these tactics many times in order to destroy his enemies completely; they were based on the enemy's strengths and formations. If the enemy openly exposed their flank and rear, and the city defenders were weak, the Mongols would encircle them from all sides. If the enemy deployed their forces by the rivers, exposing two or three flanks, then the Mongols would encircle them from all sides of the river bank.

In 1221, Chinggis destroyed Jalaldin Mangubirdi, who had deployed his soldiers on the west bank of the Indus, by attacking on two or three sides. Plano Carpini (who was in Mongolia in 1246) records that the Mongols always sent the captured personnel and non-Mongol soldiers in first, led by a few Mongols, to fight the encircled enemy. Only then would the strong regular army gradually appear from nowhere to reinforce the stronghold, outflank the enemy on both wings and then destroy them.

12 OPEN-THE-END TACTICS

If the enemy was very strong and willing to fight to the death, the Mongols would leave a gap in their ranks. In this way, the enemy might think they saw an escape route, become scattered and start to run. At that precise moment the Mongols would fix upon a suitable place to kill their fleeing enemies one by one.

13 THE COMBINATION OF SWORDS AND ARROWS TACTICS

The Mongols avoided hand-to-hand fighting if at all possible, prefering to use bows and arrows, with a range of 200 to 300 yards, to kill the enemy. Plano Carpini records:

If it is possible to avoid it, the Mongols never engage in hand-to-hand fighting. They always use arrows first to kill the enemy and their horses. After killing or wounding the enemy and their horses, making them too weak to fight, the Mongols move in to finish them off.

14 HOT PURSUIT TACTICS AND DISPERSING TACTICS

If the Mongols were winning, they would pursue the enemy so that no one escaped alive. If they were losing, however, they would disperse in all directions, so the enemy was unable to catch them.

15 BUSH CLUMP TACTICS

These tactics involved dividing the soldiers into many small groups which, although keeping contact with each other, maintained a low profile as they advanced. Such tactics were also used at night-time, and on dark or cloudy days (see Chapter Seven).

INDEX

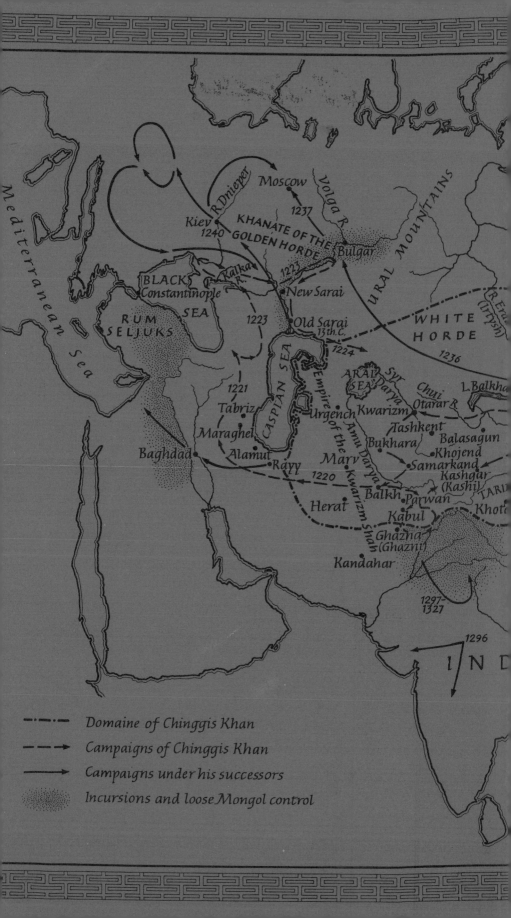

Mediterranean Sea

R. Dnieper

Moscow

1237

Volga R.

Kiev

1240

KHANATE OF THE
GOLDEN HORDE

Bulgar

URAL MOUNTAINS

Kalka R.

1223

BLACK

Constantinople

SEA

New Sarai

RUM
SELJUKS

1223

Old Sarai
13th C.

WHITE
HORDE

R. Ertis
(Irtysh)

1224

1236

CASPIAN SEA

ARAL
SEA

Syr Darya

Chui

L. Balkha

Otarar R.

1221

Empire of the

Tabriz

Urgench

Kwarizm

Tashkent

Maraghe

Bukhara

Amu Darya

Balasagun

Khojend

Baghdad

Alamut

Rayy

Marv

1220

Samarkand

Kashgar
(Kashi)

Kwarizm Shah

Balkh

Parwan

TARI

Herat

Kabul

Khot

Ghazna
(Ghazni)

Kandahar

1297-
1327

1296

IND

–·–·–·–	Domaine of Chinggis Khan
– – –▶	Campaigns of Chinggis Khan
——▶	Campaigns under his successors
⣿⣿	Incursions and loose Mongol control